hot vegan

Also by Robin Robertson

The Nut Butter Cookbook

Vegan Without Borders

Quick-Fix Vegan

More Quick-Fix Vegan

Quick-Fix Vegetarian

Vegan Planet

One-Dish Vegan

Fresh from the Vegan Slow Cooker

Party Vegan

Vegan on the Cheap

1,000 Vegan Recipes

Vegan Unplugged (co-author)

The Vegetarian Meat and Potatoes Cookbook

hot vegan

200 sultry & full-flavored recipes from around the world

robin robertson

**Andrews McMeel
Publishing**

Kansas City • Sydney • London

This book is dedicated to compassionate people
throughout the world who help each other, the animals,
and the environment by eating a healthful, plant-based diet.

CONTENTS

PREFACE

I am very pleased to present *Hot Vegan*, a new, improved incarnation of my book *Vegan Fire & Spice*, which was first published by Vegan Heritage Press in 2008. If there are two things I enjoy, it's spicy food and international cuisines. This book combines the two.

The incendiary nature of the recipes in this book is apparent, but the recipes are about much more than just heat. They're also about flavor. The recipes range from piquant to scorching, so I like to think this book has something for everyone, even if you prefer your food on the mild side. And with a selection of recipes from the various spicy cuisines all over the world, you'll never be bored.

Hot Vegan is a cookbook for all heat-seeking vegans, vegetarians, and other spicy food lovers everywhere.

WE'RE HAVING A HEAT WAVE

Long before recorded history, early humans discovered that certain seeds, barks, fruits, buds, stems, and roots had pleasingly pungent effects on the tongue. News of this flavor magic must have spread fast, because spices became so popular, people used them as money and medicine. In places where food spoiled quickly, which was just about every-where, the preserving quality of spices added to their mystique.

Camel hooves wore paths through deserts and over mountains as the Arabs built a monopoly in the spice trade all the way to India and China. From the Middle East, partic-ularly during the Crusades, spices made their way to Europe, where the Venetians built their own monopoly, and on to Britain and the New World. Today, the United States is the world's top importer of spices. Everyone loves spices to some degree, and many people thrive on them, even to obsession. Food lovers value spices as the precious seasonings that trans-form otherwise plain meals into exotic and aromatic delights.

When I was a professional chef, I worked with culturally diverse colleagues who shared their culinary knowledge and traditions. I am also fortunate to have friends from all over the world. As a result, I learned early in my career to appreciate spices and their proper use in international cuisines. Part of the fun of writing this book has been discovering delicious global fare, but especially, fare that is naturally vegan in its own right or can be easily adapted for the vegan table.

Whole grains, beans, and vegetables are ideally suited for making spicy dishes. So, while the book is not exhaustive, I have compiled what I believe to be a broad sampling of global recipes from around the world: the Americas, the Middle East, Asia, Africa, the Mediterranean, and some places in between.

With these recipes, you can transform everyday vegan meals into sultry and savory dining experiences. Most of the recipes are surprisingly easy to prepare, and will enable you to explore a wide variety of classic spicy dishes as well as some of my own interpreta-tions. Along the way, I also offer suggestions on how to enhance your cooking and define your own threshold of heat, as you explore the world of spicy cooking.

WHAT DOES SPICY MEAN?

So why do we call a particular dish "spicy"? Often paired with "hot," as in "hot and spicy," the word has erroneously come to be thought of as searingly hot. For that reason, people who don't like too much heat in their food often avoid dishes that sound "spicy," and, in the process, end up relying on the same familiar meals time and again. What the "unspiced" don't realize is that they can have "spicy" food—as in "well spiced"—without the heat anytime they wish. It comes down to adding just the right amount of seasonings to your meals to please your own palate. For the recipes in this book, you can even leave the heat out entirely, as they work just fine without any "hot stuff" at all.

Sampling meals from around the world can make cooking fun and expand your skills. It's also a great way to introduce others to vegan dining. We all know reluctant family members or friends who live in fear of being served a plain slab of tofu in place of their favorite animal part, but they're not likely to complain after sitting down to a colorful international vegan feast with piquant aromas and bold flavors. Exhilarate and intrigue them with Moroccan Vegetable Tagine with Seitan and Apricots (page 116) or Barbados-Style Grilled Kebabs (page 44), and maybe you will awaken them to the healthful, compassionate, and eco-friendly alternative of going vegan.

THE SPICES OF LIFE

I learned to love spices growing up in an Italian family. Each week, Mom made her rich, dark tomato sauce infused with fresh garlic, basil, and red wine, and sprinkled liberally with hot red pepper flakes. When I was a kid, my dad taught me the extreme sport of snacking on scorching cherry peppers right from the jar. It gave me a taste for exciting foods that inspired me later in life to explore the spicy, savory, and sometimes fiery foods of other cultures.

Most often, the fire in spicy dishes comes from chiles, and we'll look at them later. However, different kinds of heat can be achieved from a wide range of international "hot stuff" such as ginger, mustard, horseradish, and peppercorns. This book includes recipes using all these ingredients, as well as various herbs and spices that contribute to making foods well-seasoned and perhaps spicy, but not necessarily hot. Here are some of them:

Cumin—A component of both chili powder and curry powder, cumin is used in Mexico, India, the Middle East, and North Africa. Its strong, pungent, slightly bitter flavor has been used for thousands of years to season a variety of foods. Cumin seeds are yellowish brown in color. They are roasted to bring out their flavor. Cumin seeds are used either whole or ground. Whole seeds can be ground or crushed at home.

Curry: Indian, Thai, and more—Westerners tend to think of curry as the commercial curry powder found on supermarket shelves, but genuine curry powders are actually combinations of spices custom blended for specific types of dishes. The term curry is derived from the Southern Indian word for sauce: kari. Integral to the cuisines of India and Southeast Asia, curry blends can vary widely, not only among regions and countries, but also among individual cooks. Indian curry blends are usually mixtures of a dozen or more dried spices, seeds, and herbs that can include chiles, cardamom, coriander, cumin, saffron, and turmeric. They are available in both powder and paste forms. Thai and other Southeastern Asian curries, on the other hand, include mainly fresh ingredients, such as ginger, garlic, shallots, and lemongrass, and are made into pastes rather than powders.

Ginger—Hot and pungent, this root adds a distinctive flavor and bite to both sweet and savory foods. Fresh ginger is popular in Asian cuisines, while powdered ginger is used mostly in baking and spice mixtures, and is no substitute for fresh ginger when called for in savory

recipes. When purchasing fresh gingerroot, look for firm, unblemished roots.

Mustard—Available in the form of mustard seeds, mustard powder, or prepared mustard, this hot and spicy ingredient is common to a variety of world cuisines. There are forty species of mustard, and they all belong to the crucifer (cabbage) family. Mustard seeds can be found in whole, ground, or condiment form. Ground mustard is often mixed with water to form a paste. An especially hot variety is Chinese mustard. One of the most popular of the prepared mustards is Dijon, which has a rich depth of flavor. The more pungent varieties of mustard can affect the nasal passages.

Peppercorns—Black, white, and green peppercorns are obtained from the same plant by picking the berries at varying stages of ripeness. Black peppercorns, picked when the berries are half ripe, are the strongest, and are used widely on virtually every continent. (When using fresh ground pepper, add toward the end of cooking time, as it tends to lose its flavor and become bitter if cooked longer than an hour or so.) White peppercorns, the mildest, are actually black peppercorns that have had the outer skin rubbed off. Green peppercorns are undeveloped berries and are often pickled and sold in small jars. They have a fresh, piquant flavor with medium heat.

Wasabi—A member of the horseradish family, wasabi is served as a condiment with sushi in Japanese cuisine. Available in powder, or already prepared as a green paste, a little wasabi goes a long way. Add some to vegan mayo or mashed potatoes for a little culinary excitement.

CHILES BY ANY OTHER NAME

To put the "hot" in "hot and spicy," we generally look to chiles as the world's most universally popular heat source. Erroneously called chile "peppers," attributed to an error by Christopher Columbus, chiles are not peppers at all, but actually fruits. They are used in a wide variety of cuisines throughout the world in a variety of forms. You can buy them whole, fresh, dried, canned, and jarred in the form of chili oil, paste, and powder, as well as hot red pepper flakes and ground red pepper, or cayenne. Many hot condiments are made with chiles, and these include chili sauce, hot bean sauce, salsas, and various chutneys. Tabasco, a particularly popular brand of hot chili sauce, is in such wide use that it goes by its brand name.

With over a hundred varieties of chiles available, recipes calling for chiles can sometimes be confusing, especially since chiles range in heat from mildly sweet to searingly painful. Chiles are members of the capsicum family, and their heat is caused by the amount of capsaicin oil they produce, and customarily measured according to Scoville Heat Units (SHUs), a relative heat index named after Wilbur Scoville, the chemist who developed it in 1912. Here follows some of the most commonly available fresh chiles used in this book, their physical characteristics (lengths and widths are approximate), and their SHU order, ranging from the hottest (7) down to the most mild (0).

Habanero—(7) Extremely hot. Light green to bright orange. 3-inches long and 1-inch wide. Scotch Bonnets also clock in at (7).

Thai—(6) Extremely hot. Green to bright red. 2-inches long and ¼-inch wide. Dried Thai chiles are called "bird" chiles.

Cayenne—(5) Very hot. Bright red. Usually dried and ground to produce "cayenne pepper." 3- to 4-inches long and ½-inch wide.

Serrano—(4) Very hot. Deep green, bright red when ripe. 2-inches long and ⅜-inch wide.

Jalapeño—(3) Hot. Dark green. 2-inches long and ¾-inch wide. Dried, smoked jalapeños are known as chipotles and are deep red in color.

Poblano—(2) Mild to medium hot. Dark green, resembles a bell pepper. 4-inches long and 3-inches wide. Dried poblanos are anchos.

Anaheim—(1) Mild. Medium green in color. 6-inches long and 1-inch wide.

Bell Peppers—(0) Have no heat at all, and can be substituted in any recipe calling for hot chiles.

Veteran aficionados of hot food may enjoy exploring the vast world of chiles and experiment with different varieties. Chile purists would prefer to see specific names of chiles for particular uses. However, when you go to a supermarket, you may find a variety of chiles labeled simply "hot peppers." For those who don't know their serranos from their anchos, don't be discouraged. While I do call for a particular type of chile in certain recipes, I often refer to them simply as "hot" or "mild" chiles, and feel that most recipes will work just fine when one chile is swapped for another. For those who avoid heat of any kind, simply substitute sweet bell peppers for chiles, and you'll make a mild yet still flavorful dish. You may want to experiment, pick out some favorites, and stick with them.

If a recipe calls for mild, dried chiles, anchos are a good choice. For hot dried chiles, try the cayenne or Thai bird chiles. Commercial chili powders are widely available with varying degrees of quality. They are usually a blend of ground dried chiles combined with other spices, such as cumin and oregano. Paprika, the Hungarian word for "sweet pepper," refers to the powder made from ground sweet peppers. It can be labeled either "sweet" or "hot," depending on what parts of the pepper are used. When the seeds and membranes are included, or when hot varieties of chiles are also included, the result will be a "hot" paprika.

In the event that you need to make substitutions, use this list of approximate "heat" equivalents:

> 1 small, dried red chile =
> 1 tablespoon chili powder
> ½ teaspoon cayenne
> ½ teaspoon hot red pepper flakes
> ½ teaspoon hot chili paste
> 1 teaspoon Tabasco

A WORD OF CAUTION

Anyone who has engaged in hand-to-chile combat can tell you that whenever you handle hot chiles, do it very carefully. The juice or flesh of a hot chile can burn on contact, and you don't want any part of it near your eyes. Try to wear rubber or disposable gloves when handling chiles, and, if that's not possible, be sure to wash any contacted areas immediately. Whatever you do, don't rub your eyes, or anyone else's, after handling chiles.

COOLING DOWN

Fiery food lovers can be made as well as born, since we are able to build up to a tolerance for heat in our food. However, even the most ardent fire-eater needs to know how to cool down after one chile too many. Whether it be with drink, a side dish, or a dessert, putting the fire out takes a bit of know-how.

While water may be the way to put out conventional fires, you can forget about using water to tame a fire in your mouth because the capsaicin oil released from chiles is not water-soluble. Beer, wine, and creamy or fruity drinks, such as Thai iced tea or Indian mango lassi, are more effective for cooling down the inside of your mouth. Some other natural foils for hot foods are bread, pasta, rice, or other grain-based starches, which cushion the assault of our favorite incendiary dishes. Some cuisines, such as Italian, Indian, and Ethiopian, offer both grain and bread to soothe the tongue. Thai and other Asian cuisines rely on rice or noodles to soak up the heat. Many cultures include soothing dairy-based accompaniments in their cuisine, such as the Indian raita, which is made with cucumber and yogurt. Many brands of good-quality vegan yogurt are available and can be used to make "cool-down" recipes usually made with dairy yogurt. I also find fresh fruit, a cooling sorbet, or a creamy dairy-free pudding or vegan ice cream to be a perfect denouement to most spicy meals.

YOUR HOT VEGAN PANTRY

In order to produce the spicy flavors of a particular cuisine, several ingredients are generally used in combination with chiles. For example, combine chiles with cumin and tomatoes, and you have the beginning of a Mexican recipe. Chiles coupled with soy sauce and sesame oil provide flavor to Chinese and Korean recipes. Chiles paired with coconut milk or lemongrass can transport your taste buds to Thailand or Indonesia.

A well-stocked international pantry should include a variety of ingredients in order to make many of the recipes in this book. By keeping these items on hand, you will be able to prepare wholesome and delicious meals on a moment's notice. Included in your inventory should be a variety of canned and dried beans, dried and canned chiles, chili paste, capers, canned artichoke hearts, canned and sun-dried tomatoes, dried mushrooms, coconut milk, a variety of spices including good curry spice mixtures (both Indian and Thai varieties), as well as chili powder, dried fruits, oils, olives, whole grains, couscous, and pastas. And of course,

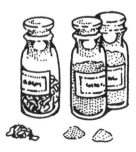

any well-stocked vegan kitchen wouldn't be without fresh seasonal produce, a supply of tofu, tempeh, and seitan, as well as soy milk, rice milk, or other dairy-free milk, and any other plant-based meat and dairy alternatives you may enjoy.

EASY SOLUTIONS
FOR EXOTIC INGREDIENTS

For the recipes in this book, my goal was to simplify recipes that normally call for truly exotic ingredients. There's nothing more frustrating than trying to make a recipe, only to realize that you have to purchase a dozen esoteric items just to get started. Wherever possible, I suggest accessible alternatives that should be available in any well-stocked supermarket. For example, in the case of Thai cooking, I suggest ginger for the traditional galangal and lime for keffir lime leaves. If I use a "borderline" ingredient (one that can be found in most but not all supermarkets) such as lemongrass, I will offer an alternative such as lemon zest in the recipe ingredient list. Additionally, some Asian cuisines traditionally use fish-based sauces, so I have included a vegan recipe for nam pla, a Southeast Asian fish sauce. While such substitutions may make some of these dishes less than authentic, the trade-off is that they enable virtually anyone to prepare exotic-tasting dishes in their own kitchen with ingredients that can be found in most supermarkets.

Seitan, Tempeh, and Tofu

Find me a vegan who has never been asked, "Where do you get your protein?" The answer, of course, is primarily from beans and grains and the foods derived from them. Wheat gives us seitan, and from soy beans come tempeh and tofu, which are all used in this book. Here are some notes for those who may be unfamiliar with them.

Seitan—Called "wheat meat," seitan is made from wheat gluten and is widely used in vegan cooking. Seitan is available in the refrigerator section of natural food stores. It can also be made at home from simple recipes found in cookbooks or online. It can be sliced, diced, or chopped for use in a variety of recipes.

Tempeh—Made from fermented soybeans that have been compressed into cakes, tempeh is available fresh or frozen in natural food stores. It makes an ideal meat alternative because of its firm texture and high protein content. Tempeh must always be eaten cooked. Because it can sometimes have a strong flavor, tempeh should be mellowed by poaching or steaming it for 30 minutes before using it in a recipe. Tempeh is especially good when marinated and can be cubed, sliced, grated, or chopped, depending on its use.

Tofu—Soybean curd that has been pressed into white cakes, tofu is available in regular or silken varieties, both of which come in textures ranging from soft to extra-firm. Widely used in Asian cooking, tofu is high in protein and calcium. It keeps for a few days in the refrigerator when covered with water. However, the water should be changed daily. It's best to use an opened package of tofu as soon as possible. Before using tofu, it should be pressed and blotted to remove excess water. Silken tofu is available in aseptic containers and may be stored without refrigeration until opened. Since tofu absorbs the flavors of the foods with which it is cooked, it is highly versatile. Silken tofu is best used to replace dairy ingredients in sauces, soups, and desserts, whereas regular tofu, which is firmer and can be sautéed, braised, fried, or grilled, works well as a meat alternative.

Vegetables

Whenever they're available, buy fresh organic vegetables that are both firm and rich in color. Be sure to wash all produce well before using, rinsing leafy greens and scrubbing other vegetables and fruits. Fresh herbs, while a welcome addition to your cooking, can be expensive. Consider growing your own herbs in a window box, even if it's just a few of your favorites. You'll be rewarded with lovely plants, as well as lively seasonings at a fraction of the price of buying fresh herbs at the supermarket. Keep plenty of garlic, ginger, and onions on hand as they store well, and are indispensable seasonings.

Cooking Oils

For general cooking, I use organic grapeseed oil, because it is neutral in taste; however safflower or sunflower oil may also be used. In addition, many recipes require the special flavors of extra-virgin olive oil or toasted (dark) sesame oil in order to succeed, and they are noted accordingly. If you wish to cut down on your intake of fats, you can substitute nonstick vegetable cooking spray, vegetable broth, or water in your cooking.

Beans: Canned or Dried?

Beans are a major staple throughout the world. They are inexpensive, easy to store and prepare, and high in protein and other nutrients. In addition to grains, beans are a mainstay of the vegan kitchen. Some people prefer to cook dried beans from scratch. If you do, consider making a double batch and freezing the extra beans for future use. Others prefer the convenience of canned beans. Available in many varieties, canned beans can be ready to use after a quick rinsing and draining. The choice is yours. I generally list "cooked or canned" beans when used as a recipe ingredient, thus allowing you to decide whether to cook the beans from scratch, pull some out of the freezer, or simply open a can.

About Vegetable Broth

A basic vegetable broth is used in many of the recipes, mainly to enhance the flavor of the dish. While a homemade broth made from fresh vegetables is best, it is not always available. If you don't have your own vegetable broth on hand, you can use canned vegetable broths or those sold in aseptic containers. You can also use a powdered vegetable base or bouillon, which you would reconstitute with water according to package directions. When choosing a commercial product, be sure to read the ingredient list to avoid any that contain monosodium glutamate or other additives. Since these products vary greatly in intensity and saltiness, be sure to check for seasonings when using these products, adding more or less salt to the recipe, accordingly. In a pinch, your "broth" can be as simple as water seasoned with a little soy sauce or miso paste. However, since vegetable broth is so easy to make, and can be portioned and frozen for convenient future use, I provide the following recipe for homemade vegetable broth:

VEGETABLE BROTH
Makes about 10 cups

Amounts and types of vegetables may be varied, but avoid strong-flavored vegetables, such as cabbage, which might overpower the broth.

1 tablespoon grapeseed oil
2 large onions, quartered (including peel)
2 celery ribs, coarsely chopped (including leaves)
3 carrots, coarsely chopped
1 potato (skin on), sliced
2 garlic cloves, unpeeled, crushed
½ cup chopped parsley (including stems)
2 bay leaves
1½ teaspoons salt
¾ teaspoon black peppercorns

Heat the oil in a large pot. Add the onions, celery, and carrots, cover and cook 5 minutes over medium heat. Add the potato, garlic, parsley, bay leaves, salt, and peppercorns. Cover vegetables with twice the amount of water. Bring to a boil, then reduce the heat to a low simmer. Simmer for an hour or more. Strain through a colander into another pot. The broth can now be used in recipes or cooled, portioned, and stored in the freezer for future use.

ABOUT THE RECIPES

As I've mentioned, you can alter the heat of a recipe by increasing or decreasing the amount of chiles, hot sauce, chili paste, or other incendiary ingredients. It's also worthy to note that you can also change the amount of any other seasonings to suit your taste. An important example is salt. Some people use salt by the grain instead of the teaspoon, while others shake it vigorously onto their food before they even taste it. The best-tasting food is usually somewhere in between. It's important to use enough salt when preparing a recipe so it has a chance to permeate the other ingredients.

Since factors such as the saltiness of your vegetable broth or other ingredients can impact how much salt you wish to use, I suggest starting with a moderate amount, and then add more to taste. That way, you can arrive at a flavor that appeals to you. For people who can't use salt for health reasons, this also applies to their salt substitute of choice.

Regarding the use of spices and herbs, a rule of thumb is to add dried herbs and spices near the beginning of a recipe so their flavors have a chance to develop, and add fresh herbs at the end so their flavors don't dissipate. Many spices are available whole and can be ground when ready to use for maximum flavor. With the exception of baking, where results depend on precision, it is my belief that most recipes should be used as guides, not inflexible blueprints. When you cook, go ahead and use a pinch more or less of a spice, and even substitute one ingredient for another, if you wish. For me, that's the fun of cooking.

BASIC KITCHEN EQUIPMENT

When you decide to journey into the realm of exotic cuisines, you shouldn't feel that you need to go out and buy special equipment. I feel that quality is better than quantity. I'd rather have a few good multipurpose pots and pans than collect a kitchen full of trendy gadgets.

Good quality, heavy stainless-steel pots and pans will get you through any recipe. You don't need a couscoussière, clay tagine, or paella pan in order to make the correlating dishes, because a good 12-inch skillet or a large saucepan will get the job done. The same skillet can be used in place of a wok for stir-fries. Of course, if you have a wok, use it. However, lightweight aluminum pans spell disaster in any language because they distribute heat unevenly, which can cause food to cook unevenly or burn. Additionally, the aluminum can leech into the food.

A set of sharp high-carbon steel knives is a worthy kitchen investment. You will also need a sturdy, flat cutting board. A food processor, a blender, and a spice mill can cut labor time dramatically.

HOW THIS BOOK IS ORGANIZED

I've organized the book into the five main geographical sections where the world's spiciest cuisines are found: The Americas, Mediterranean Europe, the Middle East and Africa, India, and Asia. Within each main section, recipes are further organized by particular countries or regions. For your convenience, each main section has its own Recipe Guide to help you quickly find recipes for appetizers, soups, salads, main dishes, and condiments. This will help you create your own great creative menus from the same cultural families or even mix them.

The recipes are also thoroughly cross-indexed in the main index at the back, with listings for all the appetizers, soups and stews, main dishes, rice and noodle dishes, salads and side dishes, sauces, condiments, and main ingredients. This allows you to either immerse yourself in a particular region's cuisine or look for an intriguing individual recipe for a less formal meal.

To further assist you in choosing recipes, super-hot dishes are marked with three chiles (🌶🌶🌶), medium-hot dishes by two chiles (🌶🌶), and mildly spicy dishes by a single chile (🌶). Many recipes do not specify a particular type of hot chile, because the heat can vary so greatly between them (see explanation of Scoville ratings in "Chiles by Any Other Name" above). For example, if you use a serrano instead of a jalapeño, the resulting dish will be much hotter. Think of these little chile symbols as more of a relative guideline and know that the actual heat level is in your own hands,

depending on the actual chiles you choose. Card-carrying chile-heads may actually want to double up. My interpretation of "hot" is one that applies to the typical Western palate. For example, even my hottest Thai recipes do not approach the incendiary heat of native Thai.

As you use this book, remember that in the wondrous world of herbs, spices, and chiles, "spicy" doesn't have to mean "hot." You can modify the degree of heat by increasing or decreasing the quantity of chiles and other hot spices that you use, all according to individual preference. For example, if you like exotic flavors, but not too much heat, simply decrease the number of chiles or eliminate them entirely. While this may render some recipes less than "traditional," they will still be flavorful and delicious.

READY FOR DEPARTURE

It's amazing to realize that in our very own kitchens, we can have the world at our fingertips. Start with some unadorned grains, beans, and fresh vegetables, and, with the mere twist of a spice mill, you can treat yourself to an astounding variety of global dishes. Whether we prefer our food mildly seasoned or searingly hot, most of us enjoy the unique flavor experiences that spices, chiles, and other seasonings have to offer.

Two of life's greatest pleasures are food and travel. While I don't travel as often as I'd like, my taste buds are veteran explorers. Whether I cook up an Indian feast, a Mexican fiesta, or a Chinese banquet, I enjoy transporting my guests to exotic areas of the globe without ever having to leave the dinner table. That's what this book is all about. It's a cooking adventure that never has to end. The richness of varied cultures can be yours for the tasting anytime you desire. For those who enjoy feasting on vegan dishes that are at once spicy, healthful, and delicious, what more could we ask?

I hope you'll think of this book as your culinary passport to the delectable spicy cuisines of the world.

ONE

❧

The Americas

RECIPE GUIDE

BLAZING TRAILS IN THE NEW WORLD

THE UNITED STATES

While known as a melting pot of nationalities and customs, the United States has been said to lack a national cuisine of its own. However, without exception, each region of the United States features a style of cooking whose roots can be traced to other areas of the globe. While many international cuisines have become popular in the restaurants of its major cities, America's own spicy cuisines have sprung up mostly in the south and southwest. In Texas, New Mexico, and California, Mexican cuisine has had the most influence on regional cooking, with its use of chiles, cumin, and other spices, for what has come to be called Tex-Mex or Southwestern cooking.

Chili con carne is believed to have originated in Texas in the late 1800s. Since that time, virtually every region of the United States has developed its own version. Another spicy, distinctly American favorite is barbecue sauce, which can be found in infinite variations.

Louisiana's spicy Cajun cooking may be the only cuisine that was actually invented in America. In addition to French and Spanish influences, the Cajuns learned about filé (ground sassafras leaves) from the Native Americans and okra from the freed African slaves. They put them together with the native rice and chiles for a cuisine that's uniquely Louisiana. The liberal use of hot pepper sauce and ground cayenne, as well as a rich dark roux, are at the heart of many intoxicatingly pungent dishes such as gumbo and jambalaya. In addition, Louisiana chefs helped spicy blackened entrées find their way to restaurant menus throughout the country.

MEXICO

Mexican cuisine is a blend of ancient indigenous and Spanish cooking, as well as other European influences. The indigenous Mexicans had long made use of the abundance of native corn, tomatoes, beans, and squash. The Spanish brought wheat, olives, and rice, and introduced citrus fruits as a way to season food. It's interesting to note that the indigenous Mexican diet was largely vegan until the Spanish introduced pork, which, along with using lard, became popular in Mexico. Chiles, however, have been cultivated in Mexico since around 7000 B.C. In addition to chiles, cumin, cilantro, oregano, garlic, and cinnamon are used to flavor many Mexican dishes.

While Mexican food is a fast-food favorite in the United States, there is far more to Mexican cuisine than the ubiquitous tacos. The use of beans, grains, and fresh vegetables in Mexican cooking makes many dishes naturally vegan, and those traditionally made with meat are easily adapted. Mexico boasts many regional specialties, where the sauces and ingredients vary greatly from each other. Compare the thick dark mole poblano, the world-famous sauce that combines chocolate and chiles, with the tangy borracho sauce that blends chiles with tequila and fruit juices.

THE CARIBBEAN

The Caribbean is home to a variety of traditions, ranging from African to Spanish, to British, Dutch, French, and East Indian. The cuisine was influenced by these varied cultures and also by the native fruits, vegetables, and spices. Allspice, cinnamon, ginger, and nutmeg are used with chiles, curry powders, peppercorns, and coconuts to season many of the island dishes. From West Africa came the popular cassavas, sweet potatoes, and plantains. In the Caribbean, beans are called peas, and black-eyed peas are a favorite. The use of rice and a colorful variety of tropical produce make island cooking vegan-friendly. The abundance of some of the hottest chiles around, such as habaneros, Scotch bonnets, and Jamaicans, helps to make this cuisine a favorite of heat-seeking people everywhere.

SOUTH AMERICA

Many South American countries boast distinguished spicy cuisines derived from ancient Indian, Spanish, and Portuguese origins. While meat is widely used throughout South America, beans, corn, rice, and quinoa (a grain native to South America) are also staple foods. Potatoes are believed to have been first cultivated in Peru, and later transplanted to Europe and North America. Many South American dishes are highly seasoned with chiles, onions, garlic, and tomatoes.

SMOKIN' TEXAS CAVIAR

Makes about 3½ cups

This protein-packed spread is delicious on crackers or can be used as a dip for corn chips or raw vegetables. The smoky heat of chipotle chiles gives it an extra kick–one chile is enough for most tastes. Black-eyed peas are popular throughout the southern United States, but they actually originated in Asia. They are used widely in China, India, and Africa.

3 cups cooked or 2 (15.5-ounce) cans black-eyed peas, drained and rinsed

¼ cup minced onion

2 garlic cloves, minced

1 or 2 canned chipotle chiles, chopped

2 tablespoons minced parsley

½ teaspoon salt

¼ teaspoon ground cumin

¼ teaspoon dried oregano

2 tablespoons olive oil

1½ tablespoons red wine vinegar

In a food processor, combine the peas, onion, garlic, chiles, parsley, salt, cumin, and oregano and pulse until just mixed, but still retaining a coarse texture. Transfer the mixture to a bowl, add the oil and vinegar, and mix well. Taste and adjust seasoning. The flavor improves if allowed to sit for an hour or so before serving.

BUFFALO CAULIFLOWER

Serves 4

Everyone's favorite crucifer is used to make these spicy plant-based Buffalo wings, served with a cooling ranch dressing for dipping. If you like lots of hot sauce, you can double up on that part of the recipe. (It freezes well, too.)

1 large head cauliflower

⅓ cup hot sauce (my favorite—and the one I use for this recipe—is Frank's RedHot Cayenne Pepper Sauce)

¼ cup vegan butter (I use Earth Balance)

2 teaspoons rice vinegar

½ cup vegan mayonnaise

1 tablespoon cider vinegar

1 tablespoon finely minced parsley (optional)

½ teaspoon onion powder

¼ teaspoon celery salt

¼ teaspoon sugar

¼ teaspoon salt

Preheat the oven to 425°F. Remove the leaves and tough core from the cauliflower. Place the cauliflower on a cutting board, cored side down, and cut it into ¼-inch thick slices, as if you were cutting a loaf of bread. Line with parchment paper, lightly oil, or spray a baking pan with cooking spray. Arrange the cauliflower slices on the baking pan. (You may need more than one pan.) Season the cauliflower with salt and pepper to taste and roast until tender and nicely browned, about 20 minutes, turning once about halfway through with a large metal spatula.

Combine the hot sauce, vegan butter, and vinegar in a small saucepan, stirring until the butter melts and the sauce is hot. Pour the sauce over the roasted cauliflower, turning to coat. Return the coated cauliflower to the oven and roast for 10 minutes longer.

In a small food processor or bowl, combine the mayonnaise, cider vinegar, parsley (if using), onion powder, celery salt, sugar, and salt. Blend until smooth. Taste and adjust the seasonings, if needed.

Serve the hot cauliflower with a bowl of ranch dressing on the side.

SPICY HOT NUTS

Makes 2 cups

There is a lot of flexibility in the type and amount of spices you use, so feel free to swap out any spice you don't love for one you do. And of course, if you're a chile-head, you can add extra cayenne.

½ teaspoon ground coriander

½ teaspoon ground cumin

½ teaspoon curry powder

½ teaspoon chili powder

¼ teaspoon ground cinnamon

¼ teaspoon ground ginger

¼ teaspoon cayenne

2 tablespoons grapeseed oil

2 cups shelled whole almonds or peanuts, pecan or walnut halves, or a combination

½ teaspoon coarse salt

Preheat the oven to 325°F. Combine the coriander, cumin, curry powder, chili powder, cinnamon, ginger, and cayenne in a small bowl. Mix well and set aside. Heat the oil in a large skillet over low heat. Add the reserved spices and cook, stirring for 2 minutes to bring out the flavors. Remove the skillet from the heat, add the nuts and stir to coat the nuts with the spices. Spread the nut mixture on a baking sheet in a single layer. Bake for 15 minutes, stirring once about halfway through. Remove from the oven, stir the nuts, and sprinkle with salt. Set aside to cool completely before storing in an airtight container.

SPICY VEGETABLE GUMBO

Serves 4

The term gumbo comes from gombo, the African word for okra, which was an original thickening agent for this robust soup. Filé powder, which is made from ground sassafras leaves, is also used to thicken and flavor gumbos. I like to use them both. Either way, a rich brown roux is essential for a good gumbo. When serving, put a bottle of Louisiana hot sauce on the table for those who like the extra kick. If okra is unavailable, add some sliced zucchini or cut green beans instead.

2 tablespoons grapeseed oil

1 green bell pepper, chopped

1 yellow onion, chopped

2 celery ribs, chopped

3 garlic cloves, chopped

2 tablespoons unbleached all-purpose flour

8 ounces okra, cut into 1-inch pieces

1 (28-ounce) can diced tomatoes, undrained

½ teaspoon dried thyme

½ teaspoon filé powder

¼ teaspoon cayenne

1 teaspoon Tabasco

3 cups vegetable broth

Salt and freshly ground black pepper

2 cups hot cooked rice

1 tablespoon minced fresh parsley

Heat the oil in a large saucepan over medium heat. Add the bell pepper, onion, celery, and garlic. Cover and cook, stirring, for about 10 minutes. Sprinkle on the flour and cook, stirring, until the flour turns light brown, about 5 minutes. Stir in the okra, tomatoes, thyme, filé powder, cayenne, Tabasco, broth, and salt and pepper to taste. Bring to a boil, then lower the heat, and simmer until the vegetables are tender, about 30 minutes. Taste and adjust seasoning. Divide the rice among four shallow soup bowls. Ladle the gumbo over the rice and sprinkle with the parsley.

CAJUN COLESLAW

Serves 4 to 6

This zesty slaw will jump-start your taste buds. The flavor improves if you allow it to sit overnight, so plan to make it the day before you need it.

1 small cabbage, cored and shredded

1 medium carrot, grated

1 garlic clove, chopped

1 fresh jalapeño, halved and seeded

2 tablespoons minced parsley

3 tablespoons red wine vinegar

1 teaspoon sugar, or a natural sweetener

¾ teaspoon salt

¼ teaspoon Tabasco

⅓ cup olive oil

In a large bowl, combine the shredded cabbage and grated carrot, and set aside. In a food processor, combine the garlic, jalapeño, parsley, vinegar, sugar, salt, and Tabasco, and process until well combined. With the machine running, slowly add the oil. Pour the dressing over the vegetables and mix well. Cover and refrigerate. Just before serving, drain the excess liquid and adjust the seasonings to taste.

RED-HOT WHITE BEAN CHILI

Serves 4 to 6

This flavorful chili pulls together quickly if you use a food processor to chop the vegetables. For extra flavor, top with some shredded vegan cheese flecked with jalapeños, available at natural food stores.

1 tablespoon olive oil

1 yellow onion, chopped

1 carrot, chopped

1 red bell pepper, chopped

2 large garlic cloves, minced

2 fresh jalapeño or serrano chiles, seeded and minced

3 tablespoons chili powder

1 teaspoon salt

½ teaspoon ground cumin

¼ teaspoon dried oregano

¼ teaspoon cayenne

⅛ teaspoon freshly ground black pepper

1 (28-ounce) can crushed tomatoes

1 cup water

4½ cups cooked or 3 (15.5-ounce) cans cannellini beans, drained and rinsed

2 scallions, minced

Heat the oil in a large saucepan over medium heat. Add the onion, carrot, bell pepper, garlic, and chiles. Cover and cook until tender, about 10 minutes. Blend in the chili powder, salt, cumin, oregano, cayenne, and pepper, and stir for 2 minutes. Add the tomatoes and water and bring to a boil. Reduce the heat to low, stir in the beans, cover and simmer until the vegetables are tender, stirring occasionally, 45 to 50 minutes. Garnish with minced scallions.

JUMPIN' JAMBALAYA

Serves 4

The term jambalaya is believed to derive from the French word jambon, which means ham. Traditional jambalaya is a rice and tomato dish made with a selection of whatever ingredients happen to be on hand. This recipe shows how well the tradition translates in a vegan kitchen. If seitan is not on hand, add more beans. Another tasty addition is sliced Tofurky sausage links. To tone down the heat, omit the chiles and cut back on the Tabasco.

2 tablespoons grapeseed oil

1 onion, chopped

1 green bell pepper, chopped

2 celery ribs, chopped

3 garlic cloves, minced

2 hot chiles, seeded and minced

1 (28-ounce) can diced tomatoes, undrained

1 teaspoon dried thyme

½ teaspoon filé powder

1 teaspoon salt

¼ teaspoon cayenne

2 teaspoons Tabasco

8 ounces seitan, cut into 1-inch pieces

1½ cups cooked or 1 (15.5-ounce) can kidney beans, drained and rinsed

Freshly cooked rice

Heat 1 tablespoon of the oil in a large saucepan over medium heat. Add the onion, bell pepper, celery, garlic, and chiles. Cover, and cook over medium heat, stirring occasionally, until softened, 5 to 8 minutes. Remove the cover, add the juice from the tomatoes, the thyme, filé powder, salt, cayenne, and Tabasco. Stir in the tomatoes and bring to a boil. Reduce the heat to low and continue to cook, stirring occasionally, for 15 minutes.

Heat the remaining 1 tablespoon of oil in a skillet over medium heat. Add the seitan and cook 5 minutes or until lightly browned, then add to the tomato mixture along with the kidney beans. Adjust the seasoning to taste and simmer an additional 10 minutes to blend the flavors. Serve over rice.

BROWN RICE WITH CREOLE SAUCE

Serves 4

This versatile sauce is also delicious on pasta or baked potatoes and makes a great "special sauce" for veggie burgers. I use brown rice instead of the traditional white rice because it is more nutritious and imparts a nutty flavor.

1½ cups long-grain brown rice, rinsed

1 tablespoon olive oil

1 green bell pepper, chopped

1 yellow onion, chopped

½ cup minced celery

1 jalapeño chile, seeded and minced

1 garlic clove, minced

1 (14.5-ounce) can diced tomatoes, undrained

1 tablespoon tomato paste

¼ teaspoon filé powder

1 tablespoon light brown sugar, or a natural sweetener

1 tablespoon lemon juice

1 tablespoon cider vinegar

1 teaspoon prepared mustard

¼ teaspoon cayenne

Salt and freshly ground black pepper

2 tablespoons minced fresh parsley

Bring 3 cups of lightly salted water to a boil. Add the rice, reduce the heat to low, cover and simmer until the rice is tender and the water is absorbed, 35 to 45 minutes.

While the rice is cooking, heat the oil in a skillet over medium heat. Add the bell pepper, onion, celery, jalapeño, and garlic. Cover and cook until softened, stirring frequently, about 10 minutes. Add the tomatoes, tomato paste, filé powder, brown sugar, lemon juice, vinegar, mustard, and cayenne and bring to a boil. Reduce the heat, add salt and pepper to taste, and simmer until the sauce thickens, stirring occasionally, about 10 minutes.

Transfer the cooked rice to a shallow bowl, top with the sauce, and sprinkle with the parsley.

TEXAS BARBECUE SAUCE

Makes about 3 cups

Although this sauce will keep well in the refrigerator for several weeks, it rarely lasts that long at my house. I use it to spice up everything from pinto beans to tofu, and it also tastes great on veggie burgers.

1 yellow onion, chopped

1 bell pepper, seeded and chopped

3 garlic cloves

2 canned chipotle chiles

1 (14.5-ounce) can crushed tomatoes

¾ cup light brown sugar, or a natural sweetener

½ cup cider vinegar

1 teaspoon salt

¼ teaspoon oregano

Combine the onion, bell pepper, garlic, and chiles in a food processor or blender and process until smooth. Add the tomatoes, brown sugar, vinegar, salt, and oregano, and process until smooth. Transfer the mixture to a saucepan and bring to a boil. Reduce the heat to a simmer, and cook, stirring frequently, for 20 to 30 minutes, or until thick. The sauce can be used immediately or allowed to cool before covering and refrigerating.

SMOOTH AND SASSY GUACAMOLE

Serves 4

Tortilla chips are the usual accompaniment, but raw vegetables and pita or bagel chips make a welcome change. Avocados were introduced to Mexico in the fifteenth century by the Incas, who originally brought them from Ecuador. I like Haas avocados because of their rich flavor and creamy texture. If you prefer a less sassy guacamole, leave out the jalapeños.

2 ripe Haas avocados
1 tablespoon fresh lime juice
½ teaspoon salt
¼ cup chopped tomato
¼ cup minced onion
1 tablespoon minced canned jalapeños
1 teaspoon minced garlic
⅛ teaspoon ground cumin

Peel and pit the avocados and place them in a food processor. Add the lime juice and salt and process until almost smooth, with a bit of texture remaining. Add the tomato, onion, jalapeños, garlic, and cumin, and blend with brief on-and-off bursts. Transfer to a serving bowl.

YUCATAN POTATO SOUP

Serves 6

The cuisine of the Yucatan varies from other regions of Mexico due to European and Caribbean influences. This flavorful soup combines potatoes and garlic with the typically Mexican cumin and tomato.

4 medium potatoes

1 tablespoon grapeseed oil

1 large yellow onion, chopped

1 garlic clove, minced

1 jalapeño chile, seeded and minced

½ teaspoon cumin

1 (14.5-ounce) can diced tomatoes, drained

3 cups vegetable broth

Salt and freshly ground black pepper

1 cup soy milk

Place the potatoes in a saucepan with enough water to cover. Boil until tender, 30 to 40 minutes. Cool the potatoes slightly, then peel, chop, and set aside. Heat the oil in a skillet over medium heat. Add the onion, garlic, and jalapeño. Cover, and cook until softened, about 5 minutes. Add the cumin and tomatoes, and simmer for 5 minutes. Allow to cool slightly.

Working in batches, combine the potatoes, tomato mixture, and 2 cups of the broth in a blender or food processor and process until smooth. Transfer to a saucepan, and add the remaining broth and salt and pepper to taste. Bring to boil, then reduce heat to low and cook, stirring constantly, for 5 minutes to heat through and blend flavors. Stir in the soy milk, adjust the seasonings to taste, and serve hot.

CHILLED AVOCADO SOUP

Serves 4

Lime juice enhances the flavor of the avocado and ensures that the soup will hold its green color for up to 2 hours.

2 ripe Haas avocados, peeled and pitted

½ cup vegan sour cream

2 tablespoons chopped fresh cilantro

1 tablespoon chopped scallion

1 teaspoon chopped garlic

1 tablespoon fresh lime juice

2 cups vegetable broth

¾ teaspoon salt

¼ teaspoon Tabasco or other hot pepper sauce

Sunflower seeds, for garnish

In a blender or food processor, combine the avocados, vegan sour cream, cilantro, scallion, and garlic. Process until smooth. Add the lime juice, broth, salt, and Tabasco and process until smooth and creamy. Refrigerate, covered, for up to 2 hours, until chilled. Serve garnished with sunflower seeds.

SPICY CORN SOUP

Serves 4

I like to garnish this creamy soup with fresh cilantro. If you want it spicier, add an extra chile.

1 tablespoon olive oil

1 medium onion, chopped

1 garlic clove, minced

1 hot green chile, seeded and minced

¼ teaspoon ground cumin

1 medium potato, peeled and cut into ¼-inch dice

3 cups water or vegetable broth

4 cups corn kernels, fresh or frozen

Salt and freshly ground black pepper

1 cup nondairy milk

2 tablespoons minced fresh cilantro or parsley, for garnish

Heat the oil in a large saucepan over medium heat. Add the onion, garlic, chile, and cumin. Cover and cook until the onion is softened, about 5 minutes. Add the potato and the water. Bring to a boil over high heat. Add the corn, reduce the heat to low and simmer until the vegetables are tender, about 15 minutes. Season to taste with salt and pepper.

In a food processor, purée 2 to 3 cups of the soup. Combine the puréed soup with the rest of the soup and let cool to room temperature. Just before serving, stir in the nondairy milk. Ladle the soup into bowls and sprinkle each serving with cilantro.

JALAPEÑO SOUP WITH TORTILLA TRIANGLES

Serves 4

The tortilla triangles add a nice crunch, as well as some relief from the heat.

1 tablespoon grapeseed oil

1 large onion, chopped

2 large garlic cloves, minced

2 jalapeño chiles, seeded and finely chopped

3 cups vegetable broth

1 (28-ounce) can crushed tomatoes

½ cup tomato sauce

2 teaspoons chili powder

½ teaspoon ground cumin

½ teaspoon minced fresh oregano or ⅛ teaspoon dried

1 teaspoon salt

2 (8-inch) flour tortillas, cut into triangles

½ cup shredded vegan cheese (optional)

Minced parsley or cilantro for garnish

Heat the oil in a large pot over medium heat. Add the onion and garlic, cover, and cook until softened, stirring occasionally, about 5 minutes. Add the jalapeños and cook until tender, stirring occasionally, about 3 minutes. Add the broth, tomatoes, tomato sauce, chili powder, cumin, oregano, and salt, and bring to a boil. Reduce the heat to low and simmer 20 minutes to blend the flavors. Preheat the oven to 400°F.

Place the tortilla triangles on a baking sheet and sprinkle with the vegan cheese, if using. Bake for 5 minutes. Ladle the soup into bowls, and garnish each bowl with tortilla triangles and parsley or cilantro.

RICE AND BEAN SALAD WITH CUMIN VINAIGRETTE

Serves 4

This colorful salad is one of my favorites because it can be made ahead of time and is hearty enough to stand as a meal in itself. Although the recipe calls for romaine, any salad greens may be substituted. For a great salad without the heat, eliminate the jalapeños.

3 cups cooked brown rice, cooled

1½ cups cooked or 1 (15.5-ounce) can pinto beans, drained and rinsed

1 cup cooked fresh or frozen corn kernels

½ medium red onion, chopped

2 tablespoons minced canned jalapeños, drained (more or less, to taste)

1 garlic clove, minced

¼ cup fresh lime juice

1 teaspoon light brown sugar, or a natural sweetener

½ teaspoon chili powder

½ teaspoon ground cumin

¾ teaspoon salt

¼ teaspoon cayenne

⅓ cup olive oil

6 cups torn romaine lettuce leaves

12 cherry tomatoes, halved

In a large bowl, combine the rice, beans, corn, onion, jalapeños, and garlic, and set aside. In a small bowl, combine the lime juice, brown sugar, chili powder, cumin, salt, and cayenne. Whisk in the oil and taste to adjust the seasonings. Pour the dressing over the salad and toss to coat. Set aside for 30 minutes at room temperature to allow the flavors to mingle.

Line salad plates with the lettuce and top with the salad mixture. Garnish with cherry tomatoes and serve.

VERACRUZ POTATO SALAD

Serves 4 to 6

Buttery Yukon Gold potatoes provide a tasty backdrop to the heat of the chiles and tang of the dressing.

1½ pounds Yukon Gold potatoes

1 small red onion, minced

1 red bell pepper, seeded and chopped

1 ripe tomato, chopped

1 serrano or other hot green chile, seeded and minced

1 tablespoon capers

¼ cup chopped fresh cilantro

3 tablespoons olive oil

2 tablespoons fresh lime juice

¼ teaspoon dried oregano

Salt

1 ripe Haas avocado

Cook the potatoes in a pot of boiling salted water until just tender, about 30 minutes. Drain and allow to cool slightly, then cut into 1-inch chunks and place in a large bowl. Add the onion, bell pepper, tomato, chile, capers, and cilantro.

In a small bowl, combine the oil, lime juice, oregano, and salt to taste. Mix well. Pour the dressing over the salad and toss gently to combine. When ready to serve, peel, pit, and dice the avocado and add to the salad.

BLACK BEAN AND CORN SALAD

Serves 4

This colorful and flavorful salad is easy to make with on-hand ingredients. For less heat, use a mild salsa. For extra heat, add some fresh or canned minced hot chiles.

1½ cups cooked or 1 (15.5-ounce) can black beans, drained and rinsed

1 cup frozen corn kernels, thawed

1 cup spicy tomato salsa

2 tablespoons chopped fresh cilantro

1 tablespoon fresh lime juice

Combine all the ingredients in a bowl and refrigerate until serving time.

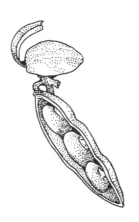

AVOCADO AND JICAMA SALAD WITH LIME DRESSING

Serves 4

The jicama, also known as the Mexican potato, is a tuber related to the sweet potato and is available in the produce section of supermarkets. Jicamas can be eaten raw or cooked and taste similar to water chestnuts. Choose jicamas that are small, firm, and have no bruises. Any fresh salad greens may be substituted for the butter lettuce.

4 tablespoons fresh lime juice

1 tablespoon orange marmalade

1 teaspoon minced lime zest

½ teaspoon salt

¼ teaspoon Tabasco or other hot pepper sauce

5 tablespoons olive oil

8 cups torn butter lettuce

1 jicama, halved lengthwise and peeled

2 ripe Haas avocados

12 cherry tomatoes, halved

12 brine-cured black olives

In a small bowl, combine the lime juice, marmalade, lime zest, salt, and Tabasco, and mix well. Whisk in the oil in a thin stream, and set aside. Line salad plates with the lettuce. Cut the jicama lengthwise into ⅛-inch-thick slices. Peel, pit, and slice the avocados. Arrange the jicama and avocado slices alternately on top of the lettuce. Top with cherry tomatoes and olives. Stir the dressing and pour over the salads.

MEXICAN FRUIT SALAD
Serves 6 to 8

While some of the elements of this colorful salad are prepared in advance and allowed to marinate, the finished salad should be served immediately once all the ingredients are combined. The use of jicama, lime juice, and pomegranate seeds makes it typically Mexican. If pomegranates are unavailable, substitute dry roasted peanuts for added texture.

2 navel oranges, peeled and cut into 1-inch chunks

2 cups fresh or canned pineapple chunks

1 jicama, peeled and cut into ¾-inch chunks

½ cup fresh orange juice

¼ cup fresh lime juice

Red leaf lettuce

2 ripe pears, cored and cut into 1-inch chunks

2 ripe bananas, sliced

Seeds from 1 pomegranate

1½ tablespoons chopped fresh mint

2 tablespoons cider vinegar

¼ teaspoon chili powder

⅛ teaspoon cayenne

1 tablespoon minced scallions

¼ cup grapeseed oil

Combine the oranges, pineapple, jicama, orange juice, and lime juice in a large bowl and refrigerate for several hours to marinate. Line a shallow bowl or large platter with lettuce leaves. Drain the marinated fruit, reserving the juice. Combine the marinated fruit with the pears and bananas, and spoon over the lettuce. Sprinkle the salad with pomegranate seeds and mint, and set aside. In a small bowl, combine ½ cup of the reserved juice, with the vinegar, chili powder, cayenne, and scallions. Whisk in the oil in a thin stream. Drizzle the vinaigrette over the salad. Serve immediately.

CHIPOTLE CORN

Serves 4

The smoky heat of the chipotle plays nicely against the sweetness of the corn.

3 to 4 cups frozen corn kernels
1 tablespoon olive oil
2 canned chipotle chile, minced
2 tablespoons minced fresh cilantro or parsley
Sea salt and freshly ground black pepper

Cook the corn according to package directions, then drain and return to the pot. Add the oil and chiles, stirring to coat. Stir in the cilantro and season to taste with salt and pepper. Transfer to a serving dish.

TACOS WITH SALSA FRESCA

Serves 4

The pinto beans can be chopped by pulsing them in your food processor. Chopped onion and vegan sour cream may also be used to top the tacos, if desired.

3 cups cooked or 2 (15.5-ounce) cans pinto beans, drained and rinsed

1 tablespoon grapeseed oil

1 ripe tomato, chopped

1 or 2 teaspoons ground chili powder

½ teaspoon ground cumin

½ teaspoon salt

¼ teaspoon freshly ground black pepper

8 corn tortillas

2 cups shredded romaine lettuce

Salsa Fresca (page 26)

Shredded vegan cheddar cheese (optional)

½ cup pitted and sliced black olives

Coarsely chop the pinto beans. Preheat the oven to 375°F. Heat the oil in a large skillet over medium heat. Add the beans, tomato, chili powder, cumin, salt, and pepper and cook for 5 minutes, stirring occasionally, until heated through. Keep warm. Wrap the tortillas in foil and warm them in the oven for 5 minutes.

To serve, place some shredded lettuce into each tortilla, and top with about ⅓ cup of the bean mixture. Garnish with Salsa Fresca, shredded vegan cheese, if using, and black olives.

SALSA FRESCA

Makes about 3 cups

Salsa adds an extra spicy touch to Mexican foods, and is a standard feature on virtually all Mexican tables. Substitute mild chiles if you want a tamer salsa.

4 large ripe tomatoes, chopped

2 serrano chiles, seeded and chopped

1 small onion, minced

2 garlic cloves, chopped

3 tablespoons fresh cilantro

¼ teaspoon freshly ground black pepper

Salt

In a bowl, combine the tomatoes, chiles, onion, and garlic. Add the cilantro, pepper, and salt, to taste. Stir to combine, then cover and refrigerate at least 1 hour before serving.

SPICY BEAN AND SPINACH BURRITOS

Serves 4

For a fresher flavor, substitute a bag of fresh baby spinach for the frozen spinach. For a milder version, omit the chile.

1½ cups cooked or 1 (15.5-ounce) can pinto beans, drained and rinsed

1 tablespoon olive oil

1 small onion, minced

2 garlic cloves, minced

1 serrano or other hot chile, seeded and minced

½ teaspoon ground cumin

½ teaspoon salt

¼ teaspoon freshly ground black pepper

1 (10-ounce) package frozen chopped spinach, thawed and squeezed dry

½ cup shredded vegan cheese (optional)

4 large flour tortillas, warmed

Tomato salsa, bottled or homemade

Place the beans in a food processor and grind coarsely with short on-and-off bursts. Set aside. Heat the oil in a large skillet over medium heat. Add the onion and garlic, cover, and cook 5 minutes, stirring occasionally. Add the chile, cumin, salt, and pepper. Stir in the spinach and reserved beans, and cook until hot, about 10 minutes.

Remove from the heat and add the vegan cheese, if using, stirring to combine well. To serve, spoon equal amounts of the filling mixture in the center of each tortilla. Top with a spoonful of salsa, to taste. Fold the bottom edge of each tortilla up over the filling, then fold the right and left sides to the center, overlapping the edges.

SALSA PICANTE

Makes about 2¼ cups

You can save time by letting your food processor do all the chopping. But be careful not to overprocess, or you may end up with spicy tomato juice.

2 large ripe tomatoes, chopped

2 tablespoons tomato paste

1 small red onion, chopped

1 serrano or jalapeño chile, halved, seeded, and chopped

1 garlic clove, chopped

1 tablespoon chopped fresh cilantro

1 tablespoon chopped fresh parsley

1 teaspoon red wine vinegar

½ teaspoon salt

In a food processor, combine the tomatoes, tomato paste, onion, chile, garlic, cilantro, and parsley, using short on-and-off bursts. Add the vinegar and salt, and mix with short on-and-off bursts until just blended, but still chunky. Transfer the salsa to a small bowl. Cover and refrigerate at least 1 hour before using.

GRILLED VEGETABLE FAJITAS

Serves 4

I especially like the chewy texture of portobello mushrooms in these fajitas. The grilled vegetables are wrapped in soft flour tortillas, and can be topped with guacamole, salsa, or the Borracho Sauce on page 36. If you don't have a grill, you can roast the vegetables in a 425°F oven.

3 portobello mushroom caps

Juice of 3 limes (about ½ cup)

3 garlic cloves, chopped

2 hot green chiles, seeded and chopped

2 tablespoons minced cilantro

1 teaspoon salt

1 yellow onion, quartered

1 red bell pepper, seeded and quartered

1 zucchini, halved lengthwise

8 flour tortillas, warmed

In a shallow bowl, combine the mushrooms, lime juice, garlic, chiles, cilantro, and salt. Cover and marinate in the refrigerator for at least 1 hour. Preheat the grill or oven. Drain the mushrooms and reserve the marinade. Place the mushrooms, onion, bell pepper, and zucchini on a grill, if using, or if using an oven, place on a baking sheet. Grill or roast the vegetables until tender and browned, basting with the reserved marinade. Slice the vegetables into thin strips and wrap up in tortillas.

SEITAN FAJITAS WITH POBLANO CHILES
Serves 4

Seitan combines with richly flavored poblano chiles to make great-tasting fajitas that can be mild to spicy, depending on the heat of the poblanos themselves, and if you add the optional red pepper flakes.

2 tablespoons olive oil

1 red onion, cut into thin strips

8 ounces seitan, cut into strips

2 poblano chiles, cut into thin strips

Juice of 1 lime

½ cup tomato salsa, bottled or homemade

¼ teaspoon hot red pepper flakes (optional)

Salt and freshly ground black pepper

4 soft flour tortillas

Heat the oil in a large skillet over medium-high heat. Add the onion, seitan, and chiles and cook until the onion and chiles are softened and the seitan is browned, about 10 minutes. Add the lime juice, salsa, and red pepper flakes, if using, and season to taste with salt and pepper. Cook 3 to 5 minutes longer to blend flavors. Divide the seitan mixture among the tortillas. Roll up and serve.

BAKED SEITAN ENCHILADAS

Serves 4

I like to use seitan in this dish, but you could use coarsely chopped pinto beans or tempeh instead, if you prefer. Warm the tortillas one at a time in a skillet or stack and wrap them in foil and warm them in a low oven. Use medium or hot salsa to increase the heat level. Serve with extra salsa and vegan sour cream.

1 tablespoon grapeseed oil

1 red onion, minced

½ green bell pepper, minced

1 hot green chile, seeded and minced

2 garlic cloves, minced

2 teaspoons chili powder

2½ cups mild tomato salsa

½ cup vegan sour cream

12 ounces seitan, chopped

8 (8-inch) flour tortillas, warmed

Preheat the oven to 350°F. Heat the oil in a large saucepan over medium heat. Add the onion, bell pepper, chile, and garlic. Cover and cook 5 minutes, or until softened. Stir in the chili powder and 1 cup of the salsa, and cook, stirring, until slightly thickened.

Remove from the heat and stir in the vegan sour cream and the seitan. Spoon about ⅓ cup of the seitan mixture onto each tortilla and roll up. Spread ½ cup of the remaining salsa in the bottom of a 9 by 13-inch baking dish. Arrange the filled tortillas in the dish. Top with any remaining seitan mixture and the remaining salsa. Cover, and bake until hot, about 20 minutes.

QUESADILLAS

Serves 4

Quesadillas are basically south-of-the-border grilled cheese sandwiches. They make a quick lunch and are also great as a snack. Serve with additional salsa and sliced avocado. Make these quesadillas as spicy as you like simply by using hot chiles and salsa instead of mild.

1 cup shredded vegan cheddar cheese

4 large flour tortillas

3 scallions, chopped

¼ cup canned chopped mild green chiles

½ cup tomato salsa, commercial or homemade

Spread the vegan cheddar cheese evenly over one half of each of the tortillas. Sprinkle the cheese with the scallions and chiles. Top with the salsa, dividing evenly among the tortillas. On at a time, place a tortilla, filling side up, in a large skillet over medium heat. Fold the tortilla in half to enclose the filling. Cook, turning once, until lightly browned on both sides. Remove the cooked quesadilla to a heatproof platter and keep warm while you cook the remaining quesadillas. To serve, place each quesadilla on a cutting board and cut it into wedges.

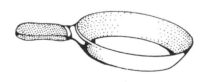

RED BEANS AND RICE CASSEROLE

Serves 4

If vegan sour cream is unavailable, you can substitute silken tofu puréed in a blender with a splash of lemon juice and a pinch of salt.

1 tablespoon olive oil

1 cup chopped onion

½ cup chopped red bell pepper

3 cups cooked brown rice

1½ cups cooked or 1 (15.5-ounce) can kidney beans, drained and rinsed

1 (14.5-ounce) can diced tomatoes, drained

1 (4-ounce) can mild chopped green chiles, drained

½ cup vegan sour cream

2 teaspoons chili powder

¾ teaspoon salt

¼ cup fine dry bread crumbs

Preheat the oven to 375°F. Heat the oil in a large skillet over medium heat. Add the onion and bell pepper, cover, and cook 5 minutes, or until softened. Transfer the onion mixture to a large bowl. Add the cooked rice, kidney beans, tomatoes, and chiles. In a small bowl, combine the vegan sour cream, chili powder, and salt, and blend well. Fold the vegan sour cream mixture into the rice and bean mixture, and mix well. Taste and adjust seasonings.

Transfer the mixture to a lightly oiled 2½-quart baking dish. Cover and bake 30 minutes or until heated through. Uncover during the last 5 minutes of baking time and sprinkle with the bread crumbs. Bake uncovered just long enough to brown the crumbs, about 5 minutes.

SEITAN
WITH TOMATO-ORANGE SAUCE

Serves 4 to 6

This dish is traditionally made with beef, but my vegan version made with seitan is simply sublime. I like to serve it over rice with a tossed salad.

2 tablespoons olive oil

¼ cup minced scallion

2 teaspoons minced garlic

½ teaspoon ground cumin

½ teaspoon hot red pepper flakes

1 (14.5-ounce) can diced tomatoes, drained

½ cup orange juice concentrate

1 teaspoon tomato paste

1 teaspoon salt

⅛ teaspoon freshly ground black pepper

1 pound seitan, cut into ¼-inch slices

Heat 1 tablespoon of the oil in a saucepan over medium heat. Add the scallions, garlic, cumin, and hot red pepper flakes. Cook, stirring for 30 seconds, then add the tomatoes, orange juice concentrate, tomato paste, salt, and pepper, and cook for 5 minutes, stirring occasionally. Taste to adjust the seasonings, and keep warm. Heat the remaining 1 tablespoon of oil in a large skillet over medium-high heat. Add the seitan and cook until browned on both sides, about 10 minutes total. Transfer the seitan to a serving platter and spoon the reserved sauce over the seitan.

RICE WITH TOMATILLOS AND CHILES
Serves 4 to 6

Tomatillos resemble small green tomatoes with papery husks. They can be found in well-stocked supermarkets and specialty grocers. If unavailable, substitute green tomatoes, or use canned tomatillos.

6 tomatillos, husked and coarsely chopped

2 small hot green chiles, seeded and chopped

2 tablespoons chopped fresh cilantro or parsley

3 cups water

1 tablespoon olive oil

½ cup minced scallions

2 garlic cloves, chopped

1½ cups long-grain white rice

1 teaspoon salt

In a blender or food processor, combine the tomatillos, chiles, cilantro, and ½ cup of the water and blend until smooth.

In a large pot, heat the oil over medium heat. Add the scallions and garlic and cook 2 minutes to soften. Add the rice and stir constantly to coat, but do not allow rice to brown. Add the reserved tomatillo purée, and simmer for 2 to 3 minutes, stirring. Add the salt and the remaining 2½ cups water, and bring to a boil, stirring once with a fork. Reduce the heat to low, cover, and simmer until the liquid is absorbed, about 30 minutes. Remove from the heat and allow to sit, covered, for 10 minutes. Fluff the rice and transfer to a serving bowl.

BORRACHO SAUCE

Makes about 2 cups

The well-known "drunken sauce" owes its flavor to the light touch of tequila. In addition to using it as a table condiment, it also makes a flavorful marinade. Agave nectar is a golden liquid sweetener. Extracted from the agave plant, it is a terrific vegan alternative to honey. Mild chiles may be used to replace the hot ones, if you prefer.

1 tablespoon olive oil
3 hot green chiles, seeded and chopped
1 small onion, chopped
1 garlic clove, chopped
¾ cup orange juice
¼ cup fresh lime juice
1 tablespoon agave nectar
⅛ teaspoon salt
¼ cup tequila

Heat the oil in a saucepan over medium heat. Add the chiles, onion, and garlic, cover, and cook for 10 minutes, or until soft. Transfer the mixture to a blender and purée with the orange juice, lime juice, agave, and salt. Return to the saucepan and cook for 10 minutes longer over medium heat. Just before serving, add the tequila.

MOLE POBLANO

Makes about 2¹/₂ cups

Perhaps the most famous and flavorful sauce of Mexico, Mole (pronounced "mo-lay") Poblano is a sublime blending of ingredients including chiles and chocolate. I use it to sauce grilled seitan or tofu, or to jazz up my veggie burgers.

2 dried ancho chiles, stemmed and seeded

2 pasilla chiles, stemmed and seeded (see note)

2 tablespoons raisins

1 tablespoon grapeseed oil

1 small yellow onion, chopped

1 garlic clove, chopped

2 ripe tomatoes, chopped

⅓ cup dry roasted peanuts

⅓ cup tortilla chips

1 tablespoon white vinegar

¼ teaspoon ground cinnamon

¼ teaspoon ground coriander

⅛ teaspoon ground cloves

1 cup vegetable broth

1 ounce unsweetened chocolate, chopped

Salt

Soak all the chiles and the raisins in a heatproof bowl with enough boiling water to cover for 1 hour to soften. Heat the oil in a skillet over medium heat. Add the onion and garlic, cover, and cook for 5 minutes, or until softened. Process the chile mixture and 1 cup of the soaking liquid in a blender until smooth. Add the onion mixture, tomatoes, peanuts, tortilla chips, vinegar, cinnamon, coriander, and cloves, and process until well blended. The mixture should be thick. Transfer the chile mixture to a saucepan, add the broth, chocolate, and salt to taste. Cook over low heat, stirring occasionally for about 40 minutes, or until the sauce is thick but pourable. If the sauce is too thick, add a little more broth. Taste and adjust the seasonings.

Note: This sauce is best when made with both ancho and pasilla chiles, but if you have difficulty finding the pasilla, simply double up on the anchos.

SPICY PLANTAIN FRITTERS

Serves 4

Plantains are synonymous with island cooking and are available in most supermarkets. I like to serve these fritters with a small bowl of chutney on the side.

1 tablespoon non-hydrogenated vegan margarine, softened

1 garlic clove, mashed to a paste

½ teaspoon light brown sugar, or a natural sweetener

½ teaspoon salt

¼ teaspoon cayenne

¼ teaspoon allspice

2 green plantains, peeled

2 tablespoons grapeseed oil

Combine the margarine, garlic, brown sugar, salt, cayenne, and allspice in a bowl and stir until smooth. Coarsely grate the plantains and combine with the mixture in the bowl, mixing until well blended. Using about ¼ cup at a time, press the mixture firmly between your palms to form tight flat patties.

Heat the oil in a large skillet over medium-high heat. Gently place the fritters into the hot oil without crowding. Fry, turning once, until golden brown and crisp, about 5 minutes total. Transfer to a heatproof platter and place in a warm oven while cooking the remaining fritters.

JAMAICAN JERK-SPICED TEMPEH NUGGETS

Serves 4

This simple and easy hors d'oeuvre also makes a great main course. The jerk spice mixture is a popular Jamaican flavor sensation and is a great way to season tempeh or seitan.

½ teaspoon garlic powder

½ teaspoon onion powder

½ teaspoon sugar or natural sweetener

½ teaspoon salt

½ teaspoon allspice

¼ teaspoon freshly ground black pepper

¼ teaspoon ground ginger

¼ teaspoon cayenne

½ teaspoon dried thyme

1 (8-ounce) package tempeh, cut into cubes

2 tablespoons grapeseed oil

Combine the garlic powder, onion powder, sugar, salt, allspice, pepper, ginger, cayenne, and thyme in a small bowl and set aside.

Place the tempeh in a saucepan of boiling water. Reduce heat to low and simmer for 30 minutes. Drain the tempeh and pat it dry.

Heat the oil in a large skillet over medium heat. Add the tempeh and cook, turning frequently, until browned on all sides, about 10 minutes. Sprinkle the spice mixture over the tempeh and toss until fragrant and evenly distributed, about 30 seconds. Serve hot.

CLOSE TO CALLALOO

Serves 4

The traditional Caribbean vegetable stew called callaloo is made with indigenous greens and seasonings that can be difficult for most of us to find at the local supermarket. This version is a close rendition using easy-to-find ingredients.

1 tablespoon olive oil

1 onion, chopped

3 garlic cloves, chopped

1 sweet potato, peeled and diced

1 red bell pepper, chopped

1 hot chile, seeded and minced

1 (14.5-ounce) can diced tomatoes, drained

1 bunch spinach, coarsely chopped

1 bunch Swiss chard, coarsely chopped

3 cups water or vegetable broth

1 (13.5-ounce) can unsweetened coconut milk

Salt and freshly ground black pepper

Heat the oil in a large pot over medium heat. Add the onion, garlic, sweet potato, bell pepper, and chile. Cover and cook until softened, 10 minutes. Stir in the tomatoes, spinach, chard, and broth and bring to a boil. Reduce heat to low and simmer until the greens are wilted. Stir in the coconut milk and season to taste with salt and pepper. Continue to cook until the vegetables are tender and the flavors are well blended, about 15 minutes.

CARIBBEAN VEGETABLE STEW

Serves 4

Stews, popular throughout the islands, often incorporate a wide variety of ingredients, as evidenced by the combination of sweet potatoes, pineapple, and olives in this dish. Serve over freshly cooked rice, millet, or quinoa.

1 tablespoon grapeseed oil

1 large onion, chopped

1 green bell pepper, chopped

1 red bell pepper, chopped

2 sweet potatoes, cut into ½-inch dice

1 hot chile, seeded and chopped

1 teaspoon minced garlic

½ teaspoon ground cumin

½ teaspoon ground cinnamon

½ teaspoon salt

1 (14.5-ounce) can diced tomatoes, drained

½ cup tomato salsa, commercial or homemade

1 (16-ounce) can pineapple chunks, with juice reserved

2 teaspoons cornstarch

1½ cups cooked or 1 (15.5-ounce) can pinto beans, drained and rinsed

½ cup pitted black olives

½ cup pimiento-stuffed green olives

Heat the oil in a large saucepan over medium heat. Add the onion, green and red bell peppers, sweet potatoes, chile, and garlic. Cover and cook for 5 minutes, or until the vegetables begin to soften. Sprinkle with the cumin, cinnamon, and salt. Add the tomatoes, salsa, and reserved pineapple juice. Cover, and simmer 20 minutes or until the vegetables are tender.

Combine the cornstarch with 2 tablespoons water and stir into the mixture. Cook, stirring, until the sauce boils and thickens, about 2 minutes. Add the pineapple, beans, and black and green olives, and heat through.

ISLAND RICE SALAD

Serves 4

The colorful variety of fresh fruits and vegetables combined with the spicy sweet chutney is especially welcome after a day in the sun.

⅓ cup chopped mango chutney

2 tablespoons fresh lime juice

¼ teaspoon ground allspice

⅛ teaspoon cayenne

3 to 4 cups cooked brown rice

1 large mango, peeled, seeded, and cut into ½-inch pieces

1 red bell pepper, finely chopped

½ cup minced celery

2 tablespoons minced scallion

Butter lettuce (or other salad greens)

Slices of mango and red bell pepper (optional garnish)

In a bowl, combine the chutney, lime juice, allspice, and cayenne, and mix until well blended. Set aside.

In a large bowl, combine the rice, mango, bell pepper, celery, and scallions. Add the reserved dressing, tossing to coat. Taste and adjust seasonings. To serve, line plates with equal amounts of lettuce, top with equal amounts of rice salad, and garnish with slices of mango and red bell pepper, if desired.

JAMAICAN-STYLE PICADILLO

Serves 4

Picadillo is a hash-like dish enjoyed throughout Latin American countries. It typically includes rice, onions, and chiles among other flavorful ingredients like almonds and olives. This version adds a touch of curry and uses black-eyed peas, although kidney beans, chopped seitan, or steamed tempeh may be used instead.

2 tablespoons grapeseed oil

1 yellow onion, chopped

1 red bell pepper, seeded and chopped

1 or 2 hot chiles, seeded and minced

2 garlic cloves, minced

2 teaspoons grated ginger

2 teaspoons curry spice blend (Jamaican-style, if possible)

1 teaspoon salt

¼ teaspoon ground cumin

¼ teaspoon dried thyme

¼ teaspoon cayenne

1 (14.5-ounce) can diced tomatoes, drained

1 (15.5-ounce) can black-eyed peas, drained and rinsed

2 cups cooked rice

½ cup frozen peas, thawed

¼ cup raisins

¼ cup slivered almonds

¼ cup water

Heat the oil in a large skillet over medium heat. Add the onion, bell pepper, chiles, garlic, and ginger. Cover and cook until softened, stirring occasionally, about 10 minutes. Stir in the curry spices, salt, cumin, thyme, cayenne, and tomatoes. Add the black-eyed peas, rice, peas, raisins, almonds, and water. Simmer, stirring frequently, until the mixture is hot and the flavors are well blended, about 10 minutes.

BARBADOS-STYLE GRILLED KEBABS

Serves 4

Coconut milk can be found in the gourmet section of most supermarkets. Be sure to soak bamboo skewers in water for 30 minutes before using to prevent burning. Serve the kebabs over freshly cooked rice.

½ cup unsweetened coconut milk

¼ cup dark rum

¼ cup grapeseed oil

½ teaspoon hot red pepper flakes

1 teaspoon minced garlic

1 teaspoon grated fresh ginger

1 large Spanish onion, quartered

1 large red bell pepper, seeded and cut into 2-inch pieces

8 ounces seitan, cut into 1½-inch cubes

2 seedless oranges, peeled and quartered

Salt and freshly ground black pepper

In a bowl, combine the coconut milk, rum, oil, hot red pepper flakes, garlic, and ginger. Place the onion, bell pepper, and seitan cubes in a shallow bowl and pour on the coconut mixture. Cover and refrigerate 2 hours, stirring occasionally.

Heat the grill, if using, or preheat the broiler. Drain the seitan and vegetables, reserving the marinade. Thread the seitan, onion, bell pepper, and orange pieces onto skewers. Season with salt and pepper, to taste. Grill or broil the kebabs, turning frequently and brushing with reserved marinade, about 8 minutes total.

JAMAICAN BAKED VEGETABLES

Serves 4 to 6

If you wish to add something "meaty" to this tropical vegetable feast, sauté chunks of seitan or steamed tempeh at the end of the cooking time and add it to the vegetables. If you have a taste for the incendiary, use a habanero or Scotch bonnet instead of the hot pepper flakes.

2 red onions, cut into 1-inch chunks

2 large carrots, cut into ½-inch slices

2 sweet potatoes, peeled and cut into 2-inch chunks

2 Yukon Gold potatoes, cut into 1-inch chunks

¼ cup water

1 cup crushed canned pineapple

¼ cup fresh lime juice

½ cup light brown sugar, or a natural sweetener

3 garlic cloves, minced

2 teaspoons grated fresh ginger

⅛ teaspoon ground cloves

½ cup orange juice

½ teaspoon hot red pepper flakes

½ teaspoon salt

¼ teaspoon freshly ground black pepper

3 tablespoons dark Jamaican rum (optional)

Preheat the oven to 425°F. Lightly oil a large roasting pan and add the onions, carrots, sweet potatoes, and white potatoes. Add the water, cover tightly, and bake for 30 minutes. In a blender or food processor, combine the pineapple, lime juice, brown sugar, garlic, ginger, cloves, orange juice, hot red pepper flakes, salt, and pepper and purée until smooth. Pour the sauce mixture over the vegetables, cover tightly, and return to the oven and bake for another 30 minutes longer. Remove from the oven and baste the vegetables with the liquid in the pan. Return to the oven and bake, uncovered, until tender, about 15 minutes longer.

When the vegetables are tender, remove from the oven and place on a serving platter. Cover loosely with foil to keep warm. Transfer the basting liquid to a small saucepan and bring to a boil over high heat. Add the rum, if using, and continue cooking, stirring constantly, for 2 minutes. Pour the sauce over the vegetables and serve.

JAMAICAN JERK SAUCE

Makes about 1¹/₂ cups

I enjoy using this aromatic sauce on everything from veggie burgers to grilled vegetables. It also makes a great marinade for tofu or tempeh, or a dipping sauce for vegetable fritters or tempura.

1 small onion, chopped
2 small hot chiles, seeded and chopped
1 garlic clove, chopped
2 tablespoons olive oil
2 tablespoons soy sauce
2 tablespoons cider vinegar
2 tablespoons molasses
1 tablespoon dark rum
1 teaspoon sugar, or natural sweetener
1 teaspoon ground allspice
½ teaspoon dried thyme
¼ teaspoon ground nutmeg

Combine all the ingredients in a food processor or blender and process until well blended. Transfer the mixture to saucepan and heat to boiling. Reduce the heat to low and simmer 10 minutes, stirring occasionally until the sauce thickens slightly.

LIME-MARINATED WHITE BEAN SALAD

Serves 4

Known as seviche or ceviche, this lime-marinated salad from Peru is traditionally made with raw fish or scallops, but cannellini or other white beans are also well suited to the zesty marinade.

1½ cups cooked or 1 (15.5-ounce) can white beans, drained and rinsed

¼ cup fresh lime juice

¼ teaspoon salt

¼ teaspoon cayenne

1 large ripe tomato, chopped

2 teaspoons minced parsley

1 scallion, minced

2 teaspoons chopped capers

¼ cup olive oil

½ teaspoon sugar, or natural sweetener

4 cups torn salad greens

Place the beans in a shallow bowl with 2 tablespoons of the lime juice, the salt, and ⅛ teaspoon of the cayenne, and toss gently to coat. Refrigerate, covered, for 1 hour.

In a bowl, combine the tomato, parsley, scallion, capers, olive oil, the remaining 2 tablespoons of lime juice, sugar, and the remaining ⅛ teaspoon cayenne and stir until well blended. Arrange the salad greens on small salad plates. Place the bean mixture on top of the lettuce and drizzle with the dressing.

QUINOA-STUFFED AVOCADOS

Serves 4

Quinoa is an ancient grain native to Bolivia and a mainstay of the Bolivian diet, along with potatoes and corn. Quinoa is available in natural food stores and well-stocked supermarkets. It makes an interesting change from rice and is also quite nutritious. Avocados are also plentiful in Bolivia and are often included in holiday feasts.

¾ cup quinoa

2 tablespoons olive oil

1 small red onion, minced

1 ripe tomato, chopped

1 serrano chile, seeded and minced

1 tablespoon minced parsley

½ teaspoon salt

¼ teaspoon freshly ground black pepper

2 ripe Haas avocados

1 tablespoon lemon juice

4 large butter lettuce leaves

Cook the quinoa according to package directions. Set aside. Heat 1 tablespoon of the oil in a skillet over medium heat. Add the onion, cover and cook for 5 minutes to soften. Transfer the onion to a bowl. Add the reserved quinoa, tomato, chile, parsley, salt, and pepper, and mix until well combined.

Carefully halve the avocados lengthwise and remove the pits. Running a small knife between the avocado skin and flesh, remove the pulp, keeping the shells intact. Cut the avocado pulp into ½-inch dice and add to the quinoa mixture. Add the lemon juice and the remaining 1 tablespoon of oil and toss gently to combine. Taste and adjust seasonings. Spoon the mixture into the reserved avocado shells and serve immediately on salad plates lined with lettuce leaves.

ARGENTINEAN-INSPIRED SEITAN CUTLETS

Serves 4

My friend Patty Gershanik is from Argentina, and her description of the ubiquitous grilled beef dishes in her native land inspired this vegan alternative. The Argentineans use lemons in a variety of dishes, and much of their cuisine has been influenced by Italian and Spanish immigrants.

⅓ cup fresh lemon juice

½ teaspoon plus ¼ teaspoon hot red pepper flakes

½ teaspoon salt, divided

¼ cup plus 2 tablespoons olive oil

8 ounces seitan, cut into ¼-inch cutlets

1 cup dried bread crumbs

½ teaspoon dried oregano

Lemon wedges, for garnish

To make the marinade, combine the lemon juice, ½ teaspoon hot red pepper flakes, ¼ teaspoon salt, and ¼ cup of the olive oil in a bowl. Arrange the seitan cutlets in a baking dish without overlapping and pour the marinade over them. Marinate for ½ hour at room temperature, or several hours in the refrigerator, turning once to spread the seasoning mixture evenly.

Place the bread crumbs in a shallow bowl. Add the remaining ¼ teaspoon red pepper flakes, ¼ teaspoon salt, and the oregano. Remove the seitan from the marinade and dredge in the bread crumbs, pressing the crumbs into the cutlets with your hands.

Heat the remaining oil in a large skillet over medium heat. Add the cutlets and cook until crisp and golden brown on both sides, turning once, 3 to 4 minutes per side. Serve with lemon wedges.

CITRUS-MARINATED TEMPEH WITH SWEET POTATOES

Serves 4

This recipe was inspired by the Peruvian dish called Chancho Adobado. I make my version with tempeh. Serve with warm flour tortillas.

2 (8-ounce) packages tempeh

1½ cups orange juice

½ cup fresh lemon juice

2 tablespoons soy sauce

1 tablespoon mirin

½ cup chopped onion

2 garlic cloves, chopped

1 hot chile, minced

1 tablespoon light brown sugar, or a natural sweetener

2 large sweet potatoes, peeled and cut into ½-inch slices

2 tablespoons grapeseed oil

1 tablespoon chopped fresh parsley

Simmer the tempeh in a saucepan of water for 30 minutes. Drain, cool slightly, then cut into ½-inch strips.

In a blender, combine the orange juice, lemon juice, soy sauce, mirin, onion, garlic, and chile, and process until blended. Transfer the marinade to a shallow bowl, add the tempeh and marinate for 1 hour. Boil the sweet potatoes until tender, about 20 minutes. Set aside to cool.

Heat the oil in a large skillet over medium heat, add the tempeh, reserving the marinade, and cook until browned all over, about 10 minutes. Reduce the heat to low and add the reserved marinade. Cover and simmer, stirring occasionally, until hot, about 5 minutes. Transfer the tempeh to a serving platter and keep warm. Add the sweet potato slices to the sauce and simmer until heated through.

Arrange the sweet potatoes around the tempeh on the serving platter. Pour on any remaining sauce and sprinkle with the parsley.

CHILEAN STUFFED PEPPERS

Serves 4

Stuffing vegetables is popular throughout the world, and Chile is no exception with this recipe for bell peppers stuffed with a spicy tomato-corn mixture.

4 large green bell peppers

2 tablespoons grapeseed oil

1 yellow onion, chopped

¼ teaspoon nutmeg

¼ teaspoon cumin

¼ teaspoon cayenne

1 (14.5-ounce) can diced tomatoes, drained

2 cups fresh or frozen corn kernels

½ cup fresh bread crumbs

¼ cup soy milk

1 teaspoon sugar, or a natural sweetener

¼ teaspoon salt

2 tablespoons dried bread crumbs

Preheat the oven to 350°F. Slice the tops off the peppers and remove the seeds. Heat 1 tablespoon of the oil in a skillet over medium heat. Add the onion, cover and cook 5 minutes, stirring occasionally until softened. Add the nutmeg, cumin, and cayenne, and cook, stirring for 1 minute. Add the tomatoes to the skillet and cook until the mixture thickens, about 3 minutes. Add the corn and mix well. Set aside.

In a small bowl, combine the fresh bread crumbs, soy milk, sugar, and salt and mix well. Add the bread crumb mixture to the skillet and mix until combined. Taste and adjust seasonings.

Fill the peppers with the corn mixture and arrange them in a baking dish. Sprinkle the dried bread crumbs over top. Drizzle the remaining 1 tablespoon of oil over the bread crumbs and add 1 cup of water to the pan. Bake for 45 minutes, or until the peppers are tender but the stuffing is still moist and lightly browned.

BRAZILIAN LEMON-CHILE SAUCE

Makes about 1¼ cups

This tangy sauce from Brazil adds a burst of flavor to everything from steamed vegetables to grilled tofu.

2 or 3 fresh hot chiles, seeded and chopped

½ cup chopped onion

2 garlic cloves, minced

½ cup fresh lemon juice

2 tablespoons chopped fresh parsley

1 tablespoon sugar, or a natural sweetener

1 teaspoon salt

Combine all the ingredients in a food processor or blender and process until blended. Let stand for 1 hour at room temperature before using or cover and refrigerate until ready to use.

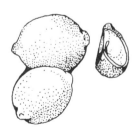

TWO

Mediterranean Europe

RECIPE GUIDE

MEDITERRANEAN HEAT

The closer to the equator you travel, the spicier the cuisine, so we'll look to the regions near the Mediterranean, notably Italy and the Iberian Peninsula, for most of Europe's "hot stuff."

ITALY

An abundance of fresh produce, herbs, and spices, along with pasta, rice (risotto), and cornmeal dishes (polenta), make Italy a vegan's culinary dream come true. Animal products are often merely used as sides or to flavor soups and sauces, so many of the classic Italian recipes are easily adapted to plant-based recipes.

Italy is home to a seemingly limitless variety of sauces, many of which are included in this book. Ironically, the tomato was actually introduced from South America, while pasta was brought to Italy from China by Marco Polo. Leave it to the Italians to bring them together for one of the most popular culinary combinations in the world. Italy's various regions boast their own specialties. Beans, particularly chickpeas, lentils, and cannellini beans, are prevalent in the food of central Italy, while the potatoes and lighter sauces of her European neighbors help color the cooking of the North. You find the spicy fare in the South, where chiles are used in combination with garlic, basil, oregano, and olives to create an irresistible savory cuisine.

While cheese is an important part of Italian cooking, authentic Italian recipes typically contain less cheese than their American interpretations, and many dishes are perfectly delicious without any cheese at all. For those who desire it, vegan versions of mozzarella and Parmesan are available to fill in the gaps. In recipes such as lasagne, tofu makes a creamy high-protein vegan alternative for the traditional ricotta cheese.

IBERIA

The Iberian Peninsula is home to Spanish, Basque, Majorcan, and Portuguese cuisines. With an eastern coastline on the Mediterranean Sea, Iberia boasts a climate similar to Italy, thus growing many of the same ingredients, such as olives and tomatoes, which lend a rich, lusty flavor to its dishes, while a judicious use of chiles keeps the heat level in the milder range.

Basques, who inhabit a region sandwiched between Spain and France, have their own cuisine, which is similar in some ways to French and Spanish cooking, with the use of mustard and peppercorns as well as olive oil, tomatoes, garlic, and numerous spices. Like the Basque people and language, their cuisine is unlike any in the world.

The food of Spain is often erroneously compared to Mexican food, when in fact it is unique and actually much closer to Italian. While Spaniards use the Mediterranean ingredients of tomatoes, garlic, chiles, and olive oil, their cooking also bears Moorish influences, hence the use of cumin, almonds, rice, and saffron. Some of the spiciest dishes of Spain come from Majorca, as well as the Catalan region.

STUFFED CHERRY PEPPERS

Serves 6 to 8

My childhood was well-spiced with appetizers such as this one, which my Italian grandmother used to make at holiday time. Now, I make them any time at all, especially for company.

2 (12-ounce) jars hot cherry peppers (about 20 peppers), drained

1 tablespoon olive oil

2 garlic cloves, minced

1½ cups fresh bread crumbs

2 tablespoons sugar, or a natural sweetener

1 cup raisins

½ cup ground walnuts

Preheat the oven to 400°F. With a small sharp knife, slice off the caps and remove the seeds from the peppers. Set aside. Heat the oil in a skillet over medium heat. Add the garlic, bread crumbs, sugar, raisins, and walnuts, and cook for 3 minutes, mixing well to combine. Pack the stuffing mixture tightly inside each of the peppers and arrange in a lightly oiled baking dish. Bake for 10 minutes or until the peppers are softened and the crumbs are browned.

PEPERONATA

Serves 4 to 6

This simple Italian dish of stewed bell peppers is best when prepared several hours in advance to allow the flavors to develop. Similar to the French ratatouille, it can be served as a first course, with crackers, or as a side dish. This is a flavorful but mild dish as is, so if you want some heat, add 1/2 teaspoon of hot red pepper flakes.

2 tablespoons olive oil

1 onion, finely chopped

1 teaspoon minced garlic

2 red bell peppers, cut into ½-inch pieces

2 green bell peppers, cut into ½-inch pieces

1 (14.5-ounce) can diced tomatoes, drained

½ teaspoon salt

¼ teaspoon freshly ground black pepper

Heat the oil in a saucepan over medium heat. Add the onion and garlic. Cover and cook for 5 minutes. Add the red and green bell peppers, and cook, uncovered, stirring occasionally, for 5 minutes. Stir in the tomatoes, salt, and pepper, and simmer until the liquid has evaporated, about 10 minutes. Remove from the heat and allow to cool slightly before serving.

SPICY OLIVES

Serves 6 to 8

You can use a combination of black and green olives, if you like. Just make sure the olives are good-quality imported olives, as they have the best flavor.

2 cups brine-cured black or green olives

Zest and juice from 1 lemon

1 tablespoon minced garlic

½ teaspoon hot red pepper flakes

½ cup olive oil

Place the olives in a bowl. Add the lemon zest and juice, garlic, and red pepper flakes. Add the olive oil, stirring to combine. Cover and set aside to marinate for an hour or two or refrigerate and marinate overnight.

GARLIC

ESCAROLE SOUP

Serves 4

My mother learned to make this soup from my grandmother who came from the Abruzzi region of Italy. I carry on the tradition at my house. The mellow cannellini beans provide the perfect balance to the flavorful broth and peppery greens.

1 tablespoon olive oil

1 yellow onion, chopped

2 carrots, chopped

1 garlic clove, minced

½ teaspoon hot red pepper flakes

6 cups water or vegetable broth

1 head escarole, chopped

2 bay leaves

½ teaspoon dried marjoram

3 cups cooked or 2 (15.5-ounce) cans cannellini beans, drained and rinsed

2 tablespoons minced parsley

Salt and freshly ground black pepper

¼ cup small, dry pasta such as pastine or orzo

Heat the oil in a large pot over medium heat. Add the onion, carrots, and garlic. Cook for 5 minutes. Add the hot red pepper flakes and the water and bring to a boil. Add the escarole, bay leaves, and marjoram, and simmer 20 minutes. Add the beans, parsley, and salt and pepper, to taste. Add the pasta and cook until tender, about 7 minutes. Remove the bay leaves before serving.

TUSCAN WHITE BEAN SOUP

Serves 4

Add some cooked pasta elbows for a delicious version of pasta e fagioli. Serve with crusty bread and a tossed green salad for a satisfying and economical meal. Place the hot red pepper flakes on the table for those who want to add more heat.

1 tablespoon olive oil

1 yellow onion, chopped

1 carrot, thinly sliced

¼ cup minced celery

2 garlic cloves, minced

1 tablespoon tomato paste

3 cups water or vegetable broth

1 (28-ounce) can crushed tomatoes

¼ teaspoon hot red pepper flakes

1 bay leaf

3 cups or 2 (15.5-ounce) cans Great Northern beans, drained and rinsed

Salt and freshly ground black pepper

3 tablespoons minced fresh basil

Heat the oil in a large pot over medium heat. Add the onion, carrot, and celery. Cover and cook until softened, about 5 minutes. Add the garlic and cook, stirring, for 1 minute. Stir in the tomato paste, water, tomatoes, red pepper flakes, and bay leaf and bring to boil. Reduce the heat to low, add the beans, and season to taste with salt and pepper. Simmer until the flavors are blended, about 30 minutes, stirring occasionally.

When ready to serve, remove the bay leaf and stir in the basil.

ITALIAN VEGETABLE RAGOUT

Serves 4

I make this hearty dish when summer's harvest is plentiful. Tomatoes, zucchini, basil, and parsley fresh from the garden make it an especially flavorful and comforting treat. Serve with crusty Italian bread, warm from the oven. If you don't have fresh ripe tomatoes, use diced canned tomatoes instead.

2 tablespoons olive oil

1 yellow onion, chopped

1 red bell pepper, chopped

3 garlic cloves, chopped

⅓ cup dry white wine

2 zucchini, halved lengthwise and cut into ½-inch slices

2 pounds fresh ripe tomatoes, chopped

½ teaspoon marjoram

¼ teaspoon hot red pepper flakes

1½ cups cooked or 1 (15.5-ounce) can cannellini beans, drained and rinsed

1½ cups vegetable broth or water

Salt and freshly ground black pepper

2 tablespoons chopped fresh parsley

2 tablespoons chopped fresh basil

Heat the oil in a large skillet over medium heat. Add the onion, bell pepper, and garlic. Cover, and cook until softened, about 10 minutes. Uncover, stir in the wine and cook until it evaporates. Add the zucchini, tomatoes, marjoram, hot red pepper flakes, cannellini beans, broth, and season to taste with salt and pepper. Cover and cook over medium heat until the vegetables are tender, about 20 minutes. Just before serving, stir in the parsley and basil.

ARTICHOKE HEARTS WITH GARLIC AND CAPERS

Serves 4

This old family recipe was always reserved for special occasion meals. I say anytime there are artichokes on the menu, that's a special occasion in itself.

1 (9-ounce) bag frozen artichoke hearts

3 tablespoons olive oil

3 garlic cloves, minced

1 tablespoon capers

½ teaspoon hot red pepper flakes

2 tablespoons fresh lemon juice

Salt and freshly ground black pepper

2 tablespoons minced fresh parsley

¼ cup toasted dried bread crumbs

Cook the artichoke hearts according to package directions. Drain and set aside.

Heat the oil in a large skillet over medium heat. Add the garlic and cook until fragrant, about 30 seconds. Add the reserved artichokes, capers, and hot red pepper flakes. Add the lemon juice and season with salt and pepper to taste. Simmer, stirring to blend the flavors for 3 minutes. Add the parsley and bread crumbs and toss to combine.

PENNE PRIMAVERA SALAD

Serves 6

Pasta primavera is normally a mild mélange of pasta and fresh vegetables, but sometimes it can benefit from a little spicing up. For this salad version, add more vegetables if you like, such as broccoli, quartered artichoke hearts, or pitted, imported olives.

1 pound penne pasta

8 ounces green beans, cut into 1-inch lengths

1 carrot, thinly sliced

6 ripe plum tomatoes, chopped

⅓ cup olive oil, plus 1 tablespoon

3 tablespoons plus 1 teaspoon white wine vinegar

Salt and freshly ground black pepper

2 garlic cloves, minced

½ teaspoon hot red pepper flakes

2 small zucchini, halved lengthwise and cut into ¼-inch slices

½ cup frozen green peas, thawed

2 tablespoons minced fresh parsley

2 tablespoons chopped fresh basil leaves

Cook the penne in a pot of boiling salted water until al dente, 10 to 12 minutes. About halfway through, add the green beans and carrot to the pasta. When the pasta and vegetables are just tender, drain and rinse under cold running water, then drain well and set aside in a large serving bowl. Add the tomatoes and set aside.

In a small bowl, whisk together the ⅓ cup of olive oil and the vinegar with about ½ teaspoon salt, and pepper to taste. Set aside.

Heat the remaining 1 tablespoon of oil in a large skillet over medium heat. Add the garlic, red pepper flakes, zucchini, and peas, and cook, stirring occasionally, for 5 minutes, then add to vegetable and pasta mixture. Pour the reserved dressing onto the pasta and vegetables. Add the parsley and basil and toss well. Set aside at room temperature for 10 minutes, then taste to adjust seasonings, adding more salt and pepper, if needed. Serve at room temperature.

ARUGULA POTATO SALAD

Serves 6

Arugula, also known as "rocket lettuce," can be eaten raw or cooked. In Italy, it is often served braised. In this recipe, arugula's piquant flavor is enhanced by the capers and cayenne in the dressing, making it an ideal complement to the potatoes. If arugula is unavailable, watercress is an excellent substitute.

1½ pounds small red potatoes, halved or quartered

Salt

1 large or 2 small red bell peppers

1 or 2 garlic cloves

1 tablespoon capers

2 tablespoons fresh lemon juice

½ teaspoon sugar

¼ teaspoon cayenne

⅓ cup olive oil

1½ cups coarsely chopped arugula

Place the potatoes in a saucepan with enough cold water to cover by 1 inch. Bring to a boil, salt the water, reduce the heat to a simmer and cook, uncovered, until the potatoes are just tender, 10 to 15 minutes. Drain well, place in a serving bowl, and set aside.

Roast the peppers over an open flame or broil about 4 inches from the heat source, turning until the skins are completely blackened. Put the charred peppers into a paper bag and let them steam for about 5 minutes to loosen the skins. Scrape off the blackened skin and remove the seeds and stems. Chop the peppers into ½-inch dice and add to the potatoes in the bowl.

Mince the garlic and capers in a food processor or blender. Add the lemon juice, sugar, cayenne, and salt, to taste, and process until well blended. With the machine running, slowly add the olive oil. Pour the dressing onto the potatoes. Add the arugula and toss until coated. Taste to adjust the seasonings, adding more salt if needed.

SWEET AND SOUR ONIONS AND ZUCCHINI

Serves 6

Whenever I can find them in the gourmet produce section of the supermarket, I like to use the delicately sweet cipollini onions. If unavailable, use small Vidalia or other sweet onions. This dish can be served hot or at room temperature.

1 pound small yellow onions, preferably cipollini, about 1½ inches in diameter

2 tablespoons olive oil

4 small zucchini, halved lengthwise and cut into ½-inch slices

Salt

3 large garlic cloves, sliced

1 bay leaf

¼ cup red wine vinegar

¼ teaspoon hot red pepper flakes

1 teaspoon sugar, or a natural sweetener

Bring a pot of water to a boil. Add the onions in their skins, bring back to a boil, and cook for 5 minutes. Drain and allow to cool, then remove the skins, leaving the onions whole.

Heat the oil in a skillet over medium heat. Add the zucchini, season with salt to taste, and cook until crisp-tender, about 5 minutes. Transfer the zucchini to a bowl.

To the skillet, add the reserved onions, garlic, and bay leaf. Cover and cook over medium heat for 20 minutes, or until the onions are tender and lightly browned. Stir in the vinegar, hot red pepper flakes, and sugar and increase the heat to medium-high, stirring until the sugar dissolves, about 2 minutes.

Pour the onion mixture over the zucchini and marinate at least 1 hour before serving. Taste and adjust seasonings. Remove the bay leaf and serve.

ROASTED POTATOES AND PEPPERS

Serves 6

This Italian potato dish is especially flavorful, owing to the final drizzle of balsamic vinegar. It's not particularly spicy, so add more red pepper flakes if you want more heat.

4 Yukon Gold or russet potatoes, peeled and cut into ½-inch slices

1 large yellow onion, halved and cut into ¼-inch slices

2 red bell peppers, seeded and cut lengthwise into ½-inch strips

½ teaspoon salt

¼ teaspoon freshly ground black pepper

¼ cup extra-virgin olive oil

1 teaspoon finely chopped fresh basil or ½ teaspoon dried

¼ teaspoon hot red pepper flakes

1 tablespoon balsamic vinegar

Preheat the oven to 400°F. Place the potatoes, onions, and bell peppers in a large roasting pan. Add the salt, black pepper, and the oil and toss to coat the vegetables. Roast, stirring occasionally, for about 45 minutes, or until the vegetables are tender. Sprinkle on the basil, red pepper flakes, and vinegar, toss to combine, and serve.

TEMPEH CACCIATORE

Serves 4

Hearty tempeh is an ideal vegan alternative to the traditional chicken in this zesty vegetable ragout.

1 pound tempeh, cut into 2-inch pieces

2 tablespoons olive oil

Salt and freshly ground black pepper

1 yellow onion, chopped

1 carrot, cut into ¼-inch slices

1 celery rib, cut into ¼-inch slices

1 green bell pepper, cut into ½-inch pieces

3 garlic cloves, minced

½ teaspoon hot red pepper flakes

½ teaspoon dried oregano

1 (28-ounce) can diced tomatoes, undrained

½ cup dry white wine

2 tablespoons minced fresh parsley

Poach or steam the tempeh for 30 minutes. Pat dry. In a large saucepan, heat the oil over medium-high heat. Add the tempeh and brown lightly on all sides, about 10 minutes. Season with salt and pepper to taste, then transfer to a plate, and set aside.

In the same saucepan, add the onion, carrot, celery, and bell pepper. Cover and cook over medium heat, until softened, 5 to 7 minutes, stirring occasionally. Add the garlic and the hot red pepper flakes and cook, stirring, for 1 minute. Add the oregano and tomatoes with their juice, and cook, stirring for 2 minutes. Add the wine and boil the mixture, stirring until it is reduced by half, about 5 minutes. Add the reserved tempeh and season with salt and pepper to taste. Bring to a boil, then reduce the heat to medium. Cover and cook for 20 minutes, then transfer the tempeh to a platter. Stir the parsley into the saucepan and spoon the sauce and vegetables over the tempeh.

ITALIAN EASTER PIE

Serves 8

Traditionally, this savory pie features hot sausage, ricotta cheese, and eggs, but, thanks to vegan sausage and tofu, I can make a plant-based version that's rich and satisfying. Called by many names in different regions of Italy, in my family it was known as Easter Pie because my mother only made it at Easter time.

2 cups unbleached all-purpose flour

¾ cup non-hydrogenated vegan margarine

¼ teaspoon sugar, or a natural sweetener

1½ teaspoons salt

¼ cup water

1 pound vegan sausage, crumbled

2 pounds firm tofu, crumbled

¼ cup grated vegan parmesan

¼ cup minced parsley

½ teaspoon freshly ground black pepper

½ teaspoon ground fennel seed

¼ teaspoon hot red pepper flakes

¼ teaspoon cayenne

¼ teaspoon paprika

Preheat the oven to 350°F. In a food processor, combine the flour, margarine, sugar, and ½ teaspoon of the salt. With the machine running, add enough of the water until a dough ball forms. Separate the dough into two equal balls, and set aside.

In a large bowl, combine the vegan sausage, tofu, vegan parmesan, parsley, remaining salt, pepper, fennel, hot red pepper flakes, cayenne, and paprika. Mix well. Taste and adjust seasoning.

Roll out the dough into two 11-inch rounds. Place the bottom crust in a 10-inch pie plate, and spread the filling mixture over it. Cover with the top crust, pinching the edges, and prick with the tines of a fork. Bake for 1 hour or until the crust is golden brown.

ZITI WITH FRESH TOMATOES AND OLIVES

Serves 4

This sauce is a summertime favorite for two reasons: it's a delicious way to feature the season's fresh ripe tomato crop, and its preparation doesn't heat up the kitchen. Another plus is that it's equally delicious served with hot or cold pasta.

2 pounds ripe tomatoes, chopped (about 4 cups)

1 cup black oil-cured olives, halved and pitted

¼ cup olive oil

¼ cup chopped fresh basil

1 tablespoon minced garlic

1 tablespoon minced fresh parsley

½ teaspoon salt

¼ to ½ teaspoon hot red pepper flakes, to taste

1 pound ziti, or other tubular pasta

Combine the tomatoes, olives, oil, basil, garlic, parsley, salt, and red pepper flakes in a bowl. Cover and let stand at room temperature for 30 minutes, stirring occasionally.

Cook the pasta in a pot of boiling salted water, until al dente, 10 to 12 minutes. Drain well and place in a large shallow bowl. Add the tomato sauce and toss gently to combine. Serve immediately, or cover and refrigerate if serving cold.

PASTA PUTTANESCA

Serves 4

This dish is named "streetwalker style" because the sauce is simply too good to resist. The classic version contains anchovies, but I think my interpretation is even more irresistible without them.

2 tablespoons olive oil

4 garlic cloves, finely chopped

1 (28-ounce) can diced tomatoes, drained

½ teaspoon hot red pepper flakes

½ teaspoon dried basil

½ teaspoon dried oregano

Salt and freshly ground black pepper

½ cup imported black olives, halved and pitted

½ cup imported green olives, halved and pitted

3 tablespoons capers, rinsed and drained

¼ cup dry white wine

1 pound spaghetti

3 tablespoons minced fresh parsley

In a saucepan, heat the olive oil over medium heat and add the garlic. When the garlic becomes fragrant, add the tomatoes, red pepper flakes, basil, oregano, and salt and pepper to taste. Bring the sauce just to a boil, then reduce heat to low, stirring to help break up the tomatoes. Simmer for 20 minutes, stirring, until the tomatoes make a thick sauce. Add the olives, capers, and wine and keep warm over low heat.

Bring a pot of salted water to a boil. Add the spaghetti to the water and cook until it is al dente, about 10 minutes. Drain the pasta and transfer to a large serving bowl.

Taste the sauce and adjust the seasonings. Add the sauce to the pasta and toss to combine. Serve immediately, sprinkled with the minced parsley.

PENNE ARRABBIATA

Serves 4

The heat in this classic Roman dish comes from the small peperoncino chiles that season the sauce. Hot red pepper flakes make a good substitute.

2 tablespoons olive oil

3 garlic cloves, minced

2 dried peperoncino chiles, crumbled or 1 teaspoon crushed hot red pepper flakes

1 (28-ounce) can crushed tomatoes

½ teaspoon dried basil

½ teaspoon dried oregano

1 teaspoon sugar, or a natural sweetener

Salt and freshly ground black pepper

1 pound penne pasta

2 tablespoons minced fresh parsley

Heat the oil in a large skillet over medium heat. Add the garlic and chiles and cook until fragrant, 1 minute. Add the tomatoes, basil, oregano, sugar, and salt and pepper, to taste. Simmer for 15 minutes to allow flavors to blend.

Cook the penne in a pot of boiling salted water, stirring occasionally, until it is al dente, about 10 minutes. Drain well and transfer to a large serving bowl. Add the sauce and toss gently to combine. Sprinkle with the parsley.

CHILE AIOLI

Makes about 1 cup

A popular alternative to butter, aioli is offered alongside the bread basket in many restaurants. This is an especially fiery version, which is also good as a dip with raw sliced vegetables or added as a final flourish to a steaming bowl of soup.

2 small dried hot chiles
4 garlic cloves
1 teaspoon salt
1 teaspoon red wine vinegar
¾ cup extra-virgin olive oil

Place the dried chiles in a bowl, pour boiling water over it, and soak until softened, about 15 minutes. Drain and place in a food processor. Add the garlic and salt and process to a smooth paste. Blend in the vinegar. With the machine running, slowly drizzle in the oil until it is emulsified. Do not overprocess. Transfer to a bowl and allow to sit at room temperature until serving time.

GARLIC SOUP

Serves 4

This brothy Spanish classic has a rich full-bodied flavor, which I find to be an amazing restorative. Try some the next time you have a cold—you'll wonder what all the fuss is about chicken soup.

2 heads garlic, separated into cloves and peeled

2 tablespoons olive oil

4 cups vegetable broth

½ teaspoon dried sage

¼ teaspoon paprika

¼ teaspoon cayenne

¼ teaspoon freshly ground black pepper

Salt

1 cup cubed French bread

3 tablespoons dry sherry

Finely mince the garlic, either by hand or in a food processor. Heat 1 tablespoon of the oil in a large saucepan over medium heat. Add the garlic and cook, stirring until softened, about 3 minutes. Do not brown.

Add the broth, sage, paprika, cayenne, black pepper, and salt to taste. Bring to a boil and simmer until the garlic is soft and mellow, about 20 minutes. While the soup is cooking, sauté the bread cubes in the remaining 1 tablespoon oil until toasted. Set aside. Add the sherry to the soup, and serve immediately, topped with the reserved croutons.

GAZPACHO

Serves 4 to 6

Many versions of the chilled Spanish vegetable soup exist—some spicy, most not. This one is somewhere in between. Omit the hot chile or add more to suit your own taste. Using a food processor cuts down on prep time considerably.

4 large ripe tomatoes, coarsely chopped

1 red onion, quartered

1 red bell pepper, seeded and quartered

1 English cucumber, peeled and quartered

1 hot chile, seeded and halved

1 cup canned regular or spicy tomato juice

¼ cup red wine vinegar

¼ cup olive oil

Salt and freshly ground black pepper

¼ cup chopped parsley, basil, dill, or cilantro (or a combination)

Place the tomatoes in a large bowl and set aside. Place the onion, bell pepper, cucumber, and chile in a food processor and pulse until well chopped, but still retaining some texture. Add the vegetables to the bowl with the tomatoes. Stir in the tomato juice, vinegar, olive oil, and salt and pepper to taste. Cover and chill 3 to 4 hours before serving. When ready to serve, stir in the parsley and taste and adjust the seasonings, if needed.

RED PEPPER AND MUSHROOM SALAD WITH WALNUTS

Serves 4 to 6

This salad is a wonderful combination of color, texture, and flavor. It is delicious by itself, though it's also great served over salad greens that have been tossed lightly with oil and vinegar.

1 teaspoon minced garlic

2 tablespoons wine vinegar

¼ teaspoon salt

¼ teaspoon sugar, or a natural sweetener

⅛ teaspoon cayenne

⅛ teaspoon dry mustard

¼ cup olive oil

3 cups sliced mushrooms

½ cup finely chopped walnuts

½ cup chopped red bell pepper

1 tablespoon minced fresh parsley

In a food processor or bowl, combine the garlic, vinegar, salt, sugar, cayenne, and mustard, and mix well. Slowly stream in the olive oil, and set aside.

In a bowl, combine the mushrooms, walnuts, bell pepper, and parsley. Pour the salad dressing over the mushroom mixture, and toss lightly to coat evenly. Allow the salad to sit for about 30 minutes before serving so the flavors can mingle.

SPANISH LENTILS

Serves 4

Whether served as a side dish or in a soup or stew, versatile lentils are a delicious source of protein.

1 tablespoon olive oil

½ cup minced onion

½ cup minced celery

1 garlic clove, minced

1 serrano or other hot chile, minced

¾ cup lentils

2 tablespoons chopped sun-dried tomatoes

3 cups water

Salt and freshly ground black pepper

2 tablespoons chopped fresh parsley

In a saucepan, heat the oil over medium heat. Add the onion, celery, garlic, and chile. Cover and cook, stirring occasionally, until the vegetables are tender, about 7 minutes.

Stir in the lentils, sun-dried tomatoes, and water. Bring to a boil, cover, reduce heat, and add salt and pepper to taste. Simmer until the lentils are tender and the liquid is absorbed, about 45 minutes. Stir in the parsley just before serving time.

SPICY SPANISH POTATOES

Serves 4

Called patatas bravas, many versions of this dish exist in Spain. This dish is recommended only for those with no fear of fire. The potatoes themselves help temper the heat of the sauce, but you'll want to be sure to pair them with a mild entrée. I sometimes serve them with scrambled tofu and toast for a Sunday brunch or light supper. Feel free to cut back on the cayenne for a less incendiary version.

1½ pounds russet or Yukon Gold potatoes, cut into 1-inch dice

2 tablespoons olive oil

2 teaspoons smoked paprika, divided

½ teaspoon cayenne, divided

Salt and freshly ground black pepper

1 (14-ounce) can fire-roasted tomatoes, well drained

1 garlic clove, crushed

2 tablespoons sherry vinegar

½ teaspoon sugar

¼ teaspoon chili powder

¼ teaspoon cumin

2 tablespoons minced fresh parsley

Preheat the oven to 425°F. In a bowl, combine the potatoes, oil, 1 teaspoon of the paprika, ¼ teaspoon of the cayenne, and salt and pepper to taste. Toss to coat. Spread the potatoes on an oiled baking sheet and roast until crisp and nicely browned, about 45 minutes, turning once about halfway through.

In a blender or food processor, combine the tomatoes, garlic, vinegar, sugar, chili powder, cumin, remaining 1 teaspoon paprika, and remaining ¼ teaspoon cayenne and process until well blended. Transfer the sauce to a small saucepan. Bring to a boil, then reduce heat to low and simmer for about 20 minutes or until thickened. Season to taste with salt and pepper. When ready to serve, combine the potatoes with the sauce in a serving bowl and sprinkle with parsley. Serve hot.

ROASTED CATALAN-STYLE VEGETABLES

Serves 4 to 6

When weather permits, try grilling the vegetables outdoors over hot coals.

2 Spanish onions, in their skins
2 red bell peppers
1 eggplant
1 head of garlic, in its skin
½ teaspoon salt
1 tablespoon capers
2 tablespoons minced fresh parsley
½ teaspoon dried marjoram
¼ cup extra-virgin olive oil

Preheat the oven to 375°F. Place the onions in a baking pan and bake for 30 minutes. Remove from the oven and add the bell peppers, eggplant, and garlic to the pan and bake 1 hour longer.

Remove from the oven and cover the vegetables with a clean dish towel for 10 minutes. Remove the charred skin from the peppers and scrape out the seeds. Cut the flesh into strips. Remove the skin of the eggplant and cut the flesh lengthwise into strips. Peel and chop the onions. Arrange the roasted vegetables in a serving dish.

Separate the baked garlic cloves from the papery skins and place in a food processor. Add the salt, capers, parsley, and marjoram and process to a paste. With the machine running, add the olive oil and process until smooth. Toss the garlic mixture with the vegetables and serve.

VEGAN PAELLA

Serves 4 to 6

Paella is traditionally made with meats and seafood, but I think there's room for a vegan version as well. I like to use Tofurky brand sausage links. If unavailable, add a can of kidney or cannellini beans to round out the dish. Saffron is authentic to paella, but the less costly turmeric will also give it a nice golden color.

1 (8-ounce) package tempeh, cut into 1-inch dice

2 tablespoons olive oil

8 ounces seitan, cut into 1½-inch pieces

8 ounces vegan sausage links, cut into 1-inch pieces

3 garlic cloves, finely chopped

½ pound green beans, cut into 1-inch pieces

1 (28-ounce) can crushed tomatoes

3 cups vegetable broth

½ teaspoon hot red pepper flakes

½ teaspoon ground fennel seed

¼ teaspoon saffron threads or ground turmeric

1½ cups short-grain rice, such as arborio

1 teaspoon salt

½ cup frozen peas, thawed

Poach or steam the tempeh for 30 minutes, and set aside. Heat the oil in a large deep skillet or saucepan. Add the seitan, sausage, and reserved tempeh, and cook for 5 minutes, turning occasionally to brown on all sides. Remove from the pan with a slotted spoon and set aside.

Add the garlic to the same pan over medium heat. Cook for 30 seconds then add the green beans, tomatoes, and broth. Bring to a boil, then stir in the hot red pepper flakes, fennel, and saffron. Reduce the heat to low, cover, and simmer for 10 minutes.

Add the rice and salt, stir well to combine, and return to a boil. Reduce the heat to low, cover, and simmer for 30 minutes or until the rice has absorbed all the liquid. Remove from the heat, add the peas, seitan, tempeh, and vegan sausage, and let stand for 10 minutes before serving.

VEGETABLES AND CHICKPEAS WITH ROMESCO SAUCE

Serves 4

The traditional Spanish romesco sauce uses a large amount of olive oil. I have pared it down considerably, and think it still tastes great. For a vibrant color contrast, add cooked frozen artichoke hearts or peas when ready to serve, just before adding the remaining sauce. The sauce is also good served over cooked grains, pasta, or crisply fried tofu.

1 yellow onion, cut into 1-inch pieces

3 tablespoons olive oil

1 small hot red chile, seeded and minced

4 garlic cloves, chopped

1 (14.5-ounce) can crushed tomatoes

2 tablespoons red wine vinegar

½ cup slivered almonds

Salt

2 red or yellow bell peppers (or 1 of each), seeded and cut into 1-inch pieces

1 eggplant, cut into 1-inch pieces

1½ cups cooked or 1 (15.5-ounce) can chickpeas, drained and rinsed

Chop 2 tablespoons of the onion and set aside. Heat 2 tablespoons of the oil in a large skillet over medium heat. Add the chile, the 2 tablespoons of onion, and 2 of the chopped garlic cloves. Cover and cook until softened, about 5 minutes. Stir in the tomatoes and vinegar and cook 10 minutes longer. Transfer the mixture to a food processor, add the almonds and salt to taste, and process until smooth. Set aside.

Preheat the oven to 425°F. In a lightly oiled 9 by 13-inch baking dish, arrange the bell peppers, eggplant, the remaining onion, and the remaining garlic. Drizzle with the remaining olive oil and season to taste with salt. Roast the vegetables until tender, about 45 minutes.

About 10 minutes before serving time, add the chickpeas to the vegetables and drizzle with about a third of the reserved sauce. Return to the oven and finish roasting the vegetables. Serve topped with the remaining sauce.

PORTUGUESE SPICY KALE SOUP

Serves 6

This healthful interpretation of a Portuguese classic tastes even better if you make it a day ahead and reheat it.

1 tablespoon olive oil

1 large Spanish onion, chopped

1 carrot, chopped

3 garlic cloves, minced

1 pound red potatoes, cut into 1-inch cubes

1 teaspoon salt

1 pound kale, trimmed and leaves torn into 1-inch pieces

½ teaspoon hot red pepper flakes

3 cups cooked or 2 (15.5-ounce) cans red kidney beans, drained and rinsed

Heat the oil in a large pot over medium heat. Add the onion and carrot, cover, and cook until softened, about 7 minutes. Add the garlic, potatoes, salt, and enough water to cover by 1 inch. Simmer for 30 minutes. Add the kale and hot red pepper flakes. Cook for 30 minutes longer. Add the kidney beans and simmer 10 minutes. Taste to adjust seasonings before serving.

BASQUE CHICKPEA STEW

Serves 4

The Basques call their homeland Euskadi. Little is known of the origin of the people or their language, but happily some of their cooking traditions lean to the spicy side.

1 tablespoon olive oil

1 large onion, chopped

1 (28-ounce) can chopped tomatoes, undrained

1 tablespoon tomato paste

2 cups vegetable broth

3 garlic cloves, minced

1 tablespoon minced fresh rosemary or 1 teaspoon dried, crumbled

1 serrano chile, seeded and minced

Salt

3 cups cooked or 2 (15.5-ounce) cans chickpeas, drained and rinsed

1 pound zucchini, cut into ½-inch pieces

Heat the oil in a large saucepan over medium heat. Add the onion, cover and cook until softened, stirring occasionally, about 5 minutes. Add the tomatoes with their juice, the tomato paste, and the broth. Add the garlic, rosemary, chile, and salt to taste, and bring to a boil. Reduce the heat to low and simmer, covered, for 30 minutes, stirring occasionally.

Add the chickpeas and the zucchini, cover, and simmer until the zucchini is tender, about 10 minutes. Taste and adjust the seasonings.

PISTO MANCHEGO

Serves 4 to 6

Originating in the La Mancha region of Spain, this "Spanish ratatouille" is especially good served with warm crusty bread. It even makes great tapas when served atop toasted bread rounds as crostini. While not especially spicy, heatwise, a touch of cayenne rounds out the flavors and adds a little kick. If fresh tomatoes are out of season, substitute a 28-ounce can of diced tomatoes.

2 tablespoons olive oil

1 yellow onion, chopped

1 small eggplant, cut into ½-inch dice

1 red bell pepper, cut into ½-inch dice

4 cloves garlic, minced

1 pound zucchini, halved lengthwise and cut into ½-inch dice

2 pounds plum tomatoes, peeled, seeded, and diced

1 tablespoon sherry vinegar

1 teaspoon minced fresh thyme

1 teaspoon salt

¼ teaspoon ground black pepper

¼ teaspoon cayenne

2 tablespoons finely chopped flat-leaf parsley

Heat the oil in a large saucepan over medium heat. Add the onion, cover, and cook for 5 minutes, until softened. Add the eggplant, bell pepper, and garlic. Cover and cook 5 minutes longer, stirring occasionally. Add the zucchini, tomatoes, sherry vinegar, thyme, salt, pepper, and cayenne.

Simmer, stirring occasionally, until all the vegetables are tender, about 30 minutes. Stir in the parsley, then taste to adjust the seasonings, if needed.

BASQUE EGGPLANT SALAD

Serves 4

The mustard in this Basque recipe shows a distinct French influence.

1 large eggplant
⅔ cup olive oil
⅓ cup red wine vinegar
1 tablespoon Dijon mustard
1 tablespoon chopped fresh parsley
1 teaspoon minced garlic
½ teaspoon salt
¼ teaspoon freshly ground black pepper
¼ teaspoon hot red pepper flakes
Butter lettuce leaves

Preheat the oven to 375°F. Cut the eggplant in half lengthwise and place it on a lightly oiled baking pan, cut side down. Bake for 30 minutes, or until tender. Allow to cool slightly, then peel and dice the eggplant into 1-inch cubes.

In a small bowl, combine the oil, vinegar, mustard, parsley, garlic, salt, pepper, and hot red pepper flakes. Place the eggplant in a shallow bowl, add the marinade, and toss to coat. Refrigerate 1 hour. Serve on lettuce leaves.

BRAISED CHICORY SALAD

Serves 4

This unusual salad of cooked greens was given to me by Marie Lange from her collection of Basque family recipes. Chicory is sometimes available as escarole or curly endive. Any of these varieties of crisp bitter greens is delicious served raw or cooked, but when served raw they are often best combined with other lettuces.

1 head chicory, end removed and
leaves separated

3 tablespoons olive oil

1 Spanish onion, sliced

2 ripe tomatoes, diced

1 teaspoon lemon juice

¼ teaspoon hot red pepper flakes

Salt and freshly ground black pepper

Wash the chicory well, then boil in salted water for 5 minutes. Drain well.

Heat the oil in a large saucepan over medium heat. Add the onion and cook until softened, 5 minutes. Add the chicory, cover, and cook until tender, about 10 minutes. Stir in the tomatoes, lemon juice, hot red pepper flakes, salt to taste, and plenty of freshly ground black pepper. Cook 10 minutes longer to allow flavors to blend. Transfer to a bowl and allow to cool. Serve cold or at room temperature.

MAJORCAN BAKED VEGETABLES

Serves 4 to 6

This Majorcan dish, known as tumbet, makes a substantial main course and needs little more than a salad and some crusty bread for a great dinner. If fresh tomatoes are out of season, use canned crushed tomatoes or a prepared tomato sauce.

2 tablespoons olive oil, or more if needed

1 pound new potatoes, sliced

2 large green bell peppers, cut into ½-inch strips

1 eggplant, cut into ¼-inch slices

4 garlic cloves, minced

1 pound plum tomatoes, chopped

½ teaspoon dried oregano

¼ teaspoon cayenne

Salt and freshly ground black pepper

Heat the oil in a large skillet over medium heat. Add the potato slices, and cook, turning frequently, for 10 minutes, or until lightly browned. Remove with a slotted spoon and set aside. Add the peppers to the oil and cook for 5 minutes, until softened. Remove with a slotted spoon and set aside. Add the eggplant to the skillet and cook in batches in the oil, until golden on both sides, adding more oil as needed. Remove and drain on paper towels.

Preheat the oven to 375°F. Add the garlic to the skillet, cook 30 seconds, then add the tomatoes, and cook for 10 minutes, stirring, to thicken. Season with the oregano, cayenne, and salt and pepper to taste.

Lightly oil a large baking dish and arrange the cooked vegetables in layers, seasoning each layer with salt and pepper. Pour the tomato sauce over the top, cover, and bake for 30 minutes or until the vegetables are tender. Let stand 10 minutes before serving.

FARCIA INTCHAUSPE

Serves 8

This spicy Basque stuffing is named for Marie Intchauspe, mother of Marie Lange and grandmother of my friend Lisa Lange. Traditionally made with chorizo sausage, Lisa and her mom, both vegans, have adapted their favorite family recipe with tofu, and enjoy it as their main course for holiday meals. It's also great with the addition of soy sausage.

2 tablespoons olive oil

2 large Spanish onions, chopped

4 ribs celery, including leaves, chopped

2 green bell peppers, chopped

2 garlic cloves, chopped

1 pound firm tofu or soy sausage, crumbled

2 large apples, chopped

1 cup chopped parsley

1 teaspoon salt

¾ teaspoon freshly ground black pepper

¼ teaspoon ground cumin

½ teaspoon dried thyme

1 teaspoon sugar, or a natural sweetener

¼ teaspoon ground sage

¼ teaspoon ground cloves

¼ teaspoon ground nutmeg

¼ teaspoon dried oregano

¼ teaspoon cayenne

¼ teaspoon turmeric

4 cups cubed bread

Preheat the oven to 350°F. Lightly oil a 9 by 13-inch baking pan. Heat the oil in a large saucepan over medium heat. Add the onion, celery, bell peppers, and garlic, cover, and cook until softened, about 10 minutes. Add the tofu, apples, parsley, salt, pepper, cumin, thyme, sugar, sage, cloves, nutmeg, oregano, cayenne, and turmeric, and cook 10 minutes longer, stirring to mix well. Add the cubed bread and mix well to combine, adding a little water or broth if the mixture is too dry. Taste and adjust seasonings. Transfer the mixture to the prepared pan. Cover and bake for 1 hour or until firm and lightly browned.

THREE

The Middle East
and Africa

RECIPE GUIDE

PUNGENT CARAVANS

THE MIDDLE EAST

The countries of the Middle East abound with spicy gastronomic pleasures. In Iran, Syria, Lebanon, and Turkey, chiles are used along with garlic, cumin, mint, fennel, saffron, and cinnamon. Traditional dishes are made with eggplant, tomatoes, artichokes, rice, couscous, and lentils, among other staples. The warm climate of the Middle East also supports a wide variety of fresh produce that includes figs, grapes, apricots, and pomegranates. Fruit is generally served with most meals, and dried fruits are a popular snack food.

AFRICA

The northern African countries that frame the southern rim of the Mediterranean Sea, such as Morocco, Tunisia, Algeria, and Egypt, enjoy foods that are more similar to the foods of Arab countries than the rest of Africa. In addition, the area of Africa above the Sahara is also quite different from the rest of the continent in cultural, economic, and social customs.

North Africa has two distinct cuisines, one in the East and one in the West. In western North African countries, such as Morocco, the heady spice mixtures used to season food can be likened to Indian food with its wide use of cinnamon, ginger, turmeric, and coriander. The North Africans also have a tradition of using fruit in their cooking. Long, slow cooking methods prevail, particularly with the tagine, which is the

name of both a Moroccan stew and the clay pot it is cooked in. The foods of eastern North Africa more closely resemble the Middle East in their uses of cumin, garlic, mint, and parsley.

Other regions of the African continent also have their traditions of spicy cuisine. This book includes delightful offerings of Ethiopia, Senegal, and Sierra Leone, all the way down to South Africa, where spicy curry dishes are popular, owing to the arrival of people from the Indian subcontinent during the nineteenth century. European influences are also apparent in South African cooking, since the British and Dutch settled there in the seventeenth century.

Grains are plentiful throughout the continent and include rice, bulgur, millet, barley, and couscous. Rice is the most common staple food, which is generally served with regional sauces. In the sub-Saharan Sahel belt, millet is the most common staple. Beans such as chickpeas, lentils, split peas, and fava beans are used throughout Africa and the Middle East to make everything from breakfast to dessert.

Because grains, beans, vegetables, and fruits are such an important part of the diet in these regions, many of the dishes are natural choices for a vegan table. I have adapted many of the native meat and seafood recipes so that the same delightfully exotic spice combinations may be enjoyed in plant-based preparations.

RED CHILE HUMMUS

Makes 2 cups

The traditional chickpea and sesame dip is enlivened by the addition of hot chiles. Tahini is the paste of ground sesame seeds widely used in Middle Eastern and Asian cooking.

2 hot red chiles, seeded and chopped

2 garlic cloves

¼ teaspoon salt

1½ cups cooked or 1 (15.5-ounce) can chickpeas, drained and rinsed

⅔ cup tahini paste

2 tablespoons fresh lemon juice

⅛ teaspoon sweet paprika

1 tablespoon chopped fresh parsley

Place the chiles, garlic, and salt in a food processor and process to a paste. Add the chickpeas, tahini, and lemon juice and process until smooth. Taste to check the seasonings, adding more lemon juice or salt, if needed. Transfer the hummus to a small bowl. When ready to serve, sprinkle with paprika and chopped parsley.

BABA GHANOUJ

Makes 2 cups

This Lebanese purée of grilled eggplant makes great party food served with crackers or pita triangles. I've seen people who dislike eggplant come back for seconds of this luscious spread.

1 large eggplant
2 garlic cloves, crushed
¼ cup fresh lemon juice
⅔ cup tahini
¾ teaspoon salt
½ teaspoon ground cumin
¼ teaspoon cayenne
¼ cup chopped parsley

Place the eggplant under a hot broiler, turning regularly until the skin is blistered all over, about 15 to 20 minutes. Place the eggplant in a paper bag or cover with a clean towel for 10 minutes. Peel off the charred skin. Squeeze the eggplant to remove the bitter juices.

Transfer the eggplant pulp to a food processor or blender, and process with the garlic, lemon juice, tahini, salt, cumin, cayenne, and parsley. Taste to adjust seasonings, adding more lemon juice or salt, if needed. Serve at room temperature.

TURKISH RED PEPPER-WALNUT SPREAD

Makes about 2 cups

Known as muhammara, this flavorful Turkish spread is wonderful slathered on triangles of pita bread. Using roasted red peppers from a jar saves time, but you can certainly roast fresh ones if you are so inclined.

2 jarred roasted red peppers, drained

¾ cup walnuts

1 garlic clove, halved

3 tablespoons olive oil

2 tablespoons fresh lemon juice

½ teaspoon hot red pepper flakes

½ teaspoon ground cumin

Salt

1 tablespoon minced fresh parsley

Combine the roasted peppers, walnuts, and garlic in a food processor and process until smooth. Add the olive oil, lemon juice, hot red pepper flakes, cumin, and salt to taste, and process until smooth and creamy. Transfer to a small bowl and sprinkle with parsley. Refrigerate until ready to serve.

MIDDLE EASTERN CHICKPEA SOUP

Serves 4 to 6

The combination of chickpeas, garlic, parsley, mint, and lemon juice is typically Middle Eastern, and makes this velvety soup uncommonly delicious. For more heat, add extra cayenne.

1 tablespoon olive oil

1 large yellow onion, chopped

2 large garlic cloves, chopped

1 bay leaf

½ teaspoon ground cumin

¼ teaspoon ground coriander

⅛ teaspoon turmeric

3 cups vegetable broth

3 cups cooked or 2 (15.5-ounce) cans chickpeas, drained and rinsed

½ teaspoon salt

¼ teaspoon cayenne

1 or 2 tablespoons fresh lemon juice

2 tablespoons minced parsley

2 tablespoons minced fresh mint

Heat the oil in a large saucepan over medium heat. Add the onion and garlic. Cover and cook until the onion softens, stirring occasionally, 5 minutes. Stir in the bay leaf, cumin, coriander, and turmeric. Cover and cook 1 minute, stirring occasionally. Add the broth and chickpeas. Cover partially and simmer for 15 minutes. Cool. Discard bay leaf.

Process the soup in a blender or food processor until smooth. Return the soup to the saucepan, and season with the salt and cayenne. Add lemon juice to taste. If the soup is too thick, add a little water. Ladle the soup into bowls and garnish with parsley and mint.

SYRIAN BEET SALAD

Serves 4

I use small young beets in this recipe because they take less time to cook than the larger ones, and are more flavorful, but you can use the larger ones if that's all you can find.

1 pound small beets

3 scallions, white part only, minced

1 garlic clove, minced

2 tablespoons chopped fresh parsley

1 tablespoon fresh lemon juice

2 tablespoons orange juice

3 tablespoons olive oil

Salt and freshly ground black pepper

Place the beets in a saucepan, cover with water, and boil until tender, about 30 minutes. When cool enough to handle, peel and dice the beets and place them in a bowl. Add the scallion, garlic, and parsley.

In a small bowl, combine the lemon juice, orange juice, and oil, and season with salt and pepper to taste. Pour the dressing over the beets while still warm, and allow to cool before serving.

TURKISH-SPICED ORANGE AND ONION SALAD

Serves 4

Many parts of the world enjoy a spiced orange salad, and the Middle East is no exception. The sweetness of the oranges balances perfectly with the pungency of the onion and salty black olives, accentuated by the gentle jolt of cayenne.

3 seedless oranges, peeled

Romaine lettuce leaves

1 red onion, cut into thin rings

8 brine-cured black olives

3 tablespoons olive oil

2 tablespoons fresh lemon juice

½ teaspoon sugar, or a natural sweetener

⅛ teaspoon cayenne

Cut the peeled oranges crosswise into ¼-inch slices and arrange on a plate lined with lettuce leaves. Scatter the onion rings over the orange slices, and scatter the olives on top.

In a small bowl, whisk together the olive oil, lemon juice, sugar, and cayenne, and drizzle over the salad.

MIDDLE EASTERN RICE SALAD

Serves 4 to 6

This colorful mélange is a feast for all the senses. When planning to make this salad, be sure to cook your rice in advance so it can be chilled before using it.

3 cups cold cooked long-grain brown rice

½ cup chopped red onion

½ cup chopped celery

¼ cup slivered blanched almonds

2 tablespoons chopped fresh mint

1 tablespoon minced crystallized ginger

1 tablespoon toasted sesame seeds

1 tablespoon minced parsley

2 seedless oranges, separated into segments and cut into bite-sized pieces

2 tablespoons orange juice

2 tablespoons fresh lemon juice

¼ cup olive oil

½ teaspoon hot red pepper flakes

¾ teaspoon salt

⅛ teaspoon freshly ground black pepper

6 cups torn romaine lettuce

In a large bowl, combine the cooked rice, onion, celery, almonds, mint, ginger, sesame seeds, parsley, and orange segments. Set aside.

In a small bowl, combine the orange juice, lemon juice, oil, red pepper flakes, salt, and pepper, and whisk until well blended. Pour the dressing over the rice mixture and toss gently to combine.

To serve, line plates with the lettuce, and spoon the rice mixture on top.

CHICKPEAS AND SWEET POTATOES

Serves 4

This vibrantly colored dish is delicious and easy to prepare. I like to serve it with couscous or rice and a dark green vegetable for a well-balanced and satisfying meal.

2 small sweet potatoes, peeled and cubed

1 tablespoon grapeseed oil

1 yellow onion, chopped

¼ teaspoon turmeric

¼ teaspoon ground cumin

¼ teaspoon ground cinnamon

¼ teaspoon cayenne

½ cup water

1½ cups cooked or 1 (15.5-ounce) can chickpeas, drained and rinsed

1 (14.5-ounce) can diced tomatoes, drained

Salt and freshly ground black pepper

Steam the sweet potatoes for 20 minutes or until just tender.

In a large skillet, heat the oil over medium heat. Add the onion, turmeric, cumin, cinnamon, and cayenne. Cover and cook for 5 minutes, stirring occasionally. Stir in the water, reserved sweet potatoes, chickpeas, tomatoes, and salt and pepper to taste. Bring to a boil, then reduce the heat to low, and simmer until the mixture thickens and the flavors are blended, about 15 minutes.

SPICY SKEWERED VEGETABLE KEBABS

Serves 4

The spicy garlic and lime marinade was just made for vegetables. The veggies are especially good served with grilled bread that has been brushed with some of the marinade. Remember to soak the wooden skewers in water for 30 minutes before using them to prevent burning. The vegetables are steamed lightly before marinating for softer, juicier results. If you prefer your vegetables crunchier, you can skip the steaming step and go directly to the marinating. Serve over hot cooked rice.

3 garlic cloves, crushed

⅓ cup grapeseed oil

¼ cup fresh lime juice

½ teaspoon ground cumin

½ teaspoon ground coriander

½ teaspoon salt

¼ teaspoon cayenne

2 small red onions, quartered

2 red or yellow bell peppers, cut into 1½-inch pieces

2 medium zucchini, cut into 1½ inch chunks

2 cups white mushrooms, trimmed, and halved or quartered if large

1 pint cherry tomatoes

Whisk the garlic, oil, lime juice, cumin, coriander, salt, and cayenne in a shallow bowl until well blended. Set aside. Steam the onions over boiling water for 1 minute. Add the bell pepper and zucchini to the steamer and continue steaming 1 minute longer. Add the mushrooms to the steamer and steam for 1 minute longer.

Transfer all the lightly steamed vegetables to the bowl with the marinade, and toss until coated. Let stand, covered, at room temperature 30 minutes, tossing occasionally.

Preheat the broiler or grill. Remove the vegetables from the marinade and thread them onto skewers, ending with a cherry tomato on each skewer. Brush with marinade and broil or grill, turning once or twice until browned, about 5 minutes.

TURKISH EGGPLANT

Serves 4

This recipe was inspired by a dish called Imam Bayildi, or "the imam fainted," supposedly because the imam, the term for a Muslim religious leader, found it so delicious. If you can't find the small eggplants, use two larger ones and cut them in quarters.

4 small eggplants

3 tablespoons olive oil

1 yellow onion, chopped

1 green bell pepper, chopped

2 garlic cloves, chopped

1 (28-ounce) can diced tomatoes, drained

¼ cup currants

1 teaspoon tomato paste

½ teaspoon ground allspice

½ teaspoon salt

¼ teaspoon cayenne

2 tablespoons sliced almonds

2 tablespoons minced fresh parsley

Preheat the oven to 375°F. Cut the eggplants lengthwise into ½-inch slices and arrange on an oiled baking sheet. Bake for 10 minutes. Set the eggplant aside to cool. Do not turn off the oven.

Heat 2 tablespoons of the oil in a skillet over medium heat. Add the onion, bell pepper, and garlic and cook until softened, 15 minutes. Add half of the tomatoes, the currants, tomato paste, allspice, salt, and cayenne. Cook for 5 minutes.

Arrange half of the eggplant slices in a single layer in a baking dish. Spread the onion mixture on top and arrange the remaining eggplant slices on top. Sprinkle the eggplant with the remaining tomatoes and scatter the almonds on top. Drizzle with the remaining 1 tablespoon of olive oil. Bake for 30 minutes or until the eggplants are tender. Allow to cool before serving. Serve garnished with the minced parsley.

RICE WITH LENTILS AND ONIONS

Serves 4

This Lebanese lentil dish is about as basic as it gets—good, simple food, delicious and economical. What could be better?

2 yellow onions

1¼ cups lentils

3 tablespoons olive oil

1½ teaspoons ground coriander

½ teaspoon ground cumin

¼ teaspoon dried marjoram

¼ teaspoon dried thyme

⅛ teaspoon cayenne

Salt and freshly ground black pepper

1 cup long-grain rice

Finely mince 1 of the onions and set aside. Cut the remaining onion in half, lengthwise, then slice each half crosswise very thinly and set aside.

Bring a large saucepan of salted water to a boil. Add the lentils and cook for 10 minutes.

Heat 1 tablespoon of the oil in a large skillet over medium heat. Add the minced onion, and cook, stirring frequently, until lightly browned, about 10 minutes.

Drain the lentils and return to the saucepan. Add the cooked onion, coriander, cumin, marjoram, thyme, cayenne, and salt and pepper to taste. Add the rice and 3 cups of water and bring to a boil. Cook uncovered for about 30 minutes or until the lentils and rice are tender. Reduce the heat to low, cover, and set aside for 10 minutes.

Heat the remaining 2 tablespoons of oil in a skillet over medium-high heat. Add the sliced onion and cook, stirring frequently, until brown and caramelized, about 15 minutes. Put the rice and lentil mixture in a large bowl, sprinkle with the fried onions, and serve.

STUFFED TOMATOES WITH CURRANTS AND PINE NUTS

Serves 4

This stuffed tomato recipe is known as yalanchi in the Middle East. You can also use the filling to stuff eggplant, squash, or grape leaves, if you prefer.

4 large, firm, ripe tomatoes

Salt

2 tablespoons olive oil

1 yellow onion, chopped

½ cup currants or raisins, soaked in warm water for 10 minutes and drained

¼ cup pine nuts

2 tablespoons minced fresh parsley

¼ teaspoon ground allspice

¼ teaspoon freshly ground black pepper

½ teaspoon sweet paprika

¼ teaspoon ground cinnamon

¼ teaspoon cayenne

1 tablespoon fresh lemon juice

3 cups cooked rice

¼ cup dry white wine

Preheat the oven to 350°F. Lightly oil a shallow baking dish and set aside. Slice off the tomato tops and scoop out the pulp. Lightly sprinkle the insides of the tomatoes with salt, and invert onto paper towels to drain.

Heat 1 tablespoon of the oil in a large skillet over medium heat. Add the onion, cover, and cook for 5 minutes, or until softened. Add the currants, pine nuts, parsley, allspice, pepper, paprika, cinnamon, and cayenne, stirring to combine. Transfer the mixture to a bowl, add the lemon juice and rice, and mix well.

Stuff the mixture into the tomatoes and arrange them in the prepared baking dish. Drizzle with the remaining 1 tablespoon oil, and the white wine. Bake for 30 minutes or until the tomatoes are hot and the stuffing is lightly browned.

PERSIAN ORANGE RICE WITH PISTACHIOS

Serves 4

At once fruity and spicy, redolent of oranges, garlic, ginger, and cinnamon, this aromatic rice dish is a sublime blending of colors and flavors, and makes a lovely addition to a buffet table.

2 large seedless oranges

2 garlic cloves, minced

1 tablespoon grated fresh ginger

½ teaspoon hot red pepper flakes

½ teaspoon ground cinnamon

¼ teaspoon turmeric

¼ cup frozen orange juice concentrate

1 teaspoon sugar, or a natural sweetener

2 tablespoons grapeseed oil

½ cup vegetable broth

4 cups cooked brown rice

½ cup chopped pistachios

¼ cup minced fresh parsley

Salt and freshly ground black pepper

Grate the oranges to remove the zest. Blanch the orange zest in boiling water for 1 minute, then set aside. Peel and chop the oranges.

In a blender, combine the oranges, garlic, ginger, hot red pepper flakes, cinnamon, turmeric, orange juice, and sugar, and blend until smooth.

Heat the oil in a large skillet over low heat. Add the reserved orange zest and gently saute for 1 minute. Add the contents of the blender and the broth and simmer, stirring occasionally, for 5 minutes.

Add the cooked rice and stir gently to heat through. Add the pistachios and parsley, and continue to cook, stirring gently, until hot. Season to taste with salt and pepper. Transfer to a serving dish and serve hot.

TURKISH BULGUR PILAF

Serves 4

Made from wheat kernels, bulgur is said to have originated thousands of years ago in Syria. It has a hearty, nutty flavor, and like couscous, it takes only a few minutes to prepare.

¾ cup medium bulgur (cracked wheat)

2 tablespoons grapeseed oil

2 carrots, cut into ¼-inch dice

1 yellow onion, chopped

1 teaspoon salt

¼ teaspoon cayenne

1 cup vegetable broth

1 cup frozen green peas, thawed

¼ cup coarsely chopped walnut pieces

¼ cup raisins

1 tablespoon chopped fresh mint

Place the bulgur in large bowl and cover with water. Drain the bulgur and set aside.

Heat the oil in a saucepan over medium heat. Add the carrots and onion, cover, and cook, stirring occasionally until softened, about 5 minutes. Add the bulgur, salt, and cayenne, and stir until the bulgur is well coated with oil, about 1 minute. Add the broth and heat to boiling. Reduce the heat to low, cover, and simmer until the bulgur is tender and the liquid has been absorbed, about 10 minutes. Add the peas, walnuts, and raisins and set aside covered 5 minutes longer.

Transfer the bulgur to a serving bowl, fluff with a fork, and sprinkle with the mint.

BULGUR-STUFFED PEPPERS

Serves 4 to 6

The hearty spicy bulgur mixture makes a scrumptious stuffing for bell peppers, although it's quite delicious served on its own as well.

1 cup bulgur

2½ cups water

Salt

4 to 6 green bell peppers

2 tablespoons olive oil

1 yellow onion, chopped

½ cup chopped celery

2 garlic cloves, minced

2 small fresh hot chiles, seeded and minced

¼ cup minced fresh parsley

1 tablespoon minced fresh dill or 1 teaspoon dried dill

½ teaspoon ground cumin

2 tablespoons fresh lemon juice

¼ cup pine nuts

¼ cup currants

1 teaspoon sugar, or a natural sweetener

Freshly ground black pepper

Preheat the oven to 350°F. Combine the bulgur and 2 cups of the water in a saucepan and bring to a boil. Reduce the heat to low, salt the water, then cover and cook for 15 minutes. Set aside to cool. In a pot of boiling water, blanch the peppers for 5 minutes, or until softened. Remove from the water and allow to cool.

Heat the oil in a large skillet over medium heat. Add the onion, celery, garlic, and chiles, and cook 5 minutes, or until softened. Add the parsley, dill, cumin, lemon juice, pine nuts, currants, sugar, reserved bulgur, and salt and pepper to taste, and mix well.

Gently stuff the mixture into the peppers and arrange them in a baking dish. Add the remaining ½ cup of water to the bottom of the dish. Cover and bake for 30 minutes or until the peppers are tender.

GARLIC MINT SAUCE

Makes about 2½ cups

For a great fusion dish, toss this Middle Eastern "pesto" with cooked pasta, or use it as a dipping sauce for steamed green beans or fried tofu cubes. It's also good tossed with rice, couscous, or potatoes, for a refreshing change of pace.

2 cups fresh bread crumbs

1 cup cold water

5 medium garlic cloves

½ teaspoon salt

¾ cup ground walnuts

¼ cup chopped fresh mint

¼ cup white wine vinegar

½ cup olive oil

½ cup warm water

Place the bread crumbs in a bowl. Add the 1 cup cold water and let stand until absorbed, about 3 minutes. Squeeze any excess liquid from the crumbs. Discard the liquid and reserve the crumbs.

Grind the garlic and salt to a paste in a food processor. Add the walnuts and mint, and process finely. Add the reserved bread crumbs and the vinegar and blend until a paste forms. With the machine running, slowly add the oil through the feed tube and blend until smooth. Add enough of the warm water, as needed, to form a thick sauce.

MINT

ORANGE GINGER DRESSING

Makes about 1 cup

This is an exotic and creamy dressing that is ideal tossed with a green salad and is especially good with a Middle Eastern or Indian meal.

⅓ cup frozen orange juice concentrate

½ cup vegan yogurt or soft silken tofu

1 tablespoon fresh lemon juice

1 teaspoon finely grated fresh ginger

¼ teaspoon ground cumin

⅛ teaspoon cayenne

⅛ teaspoon ground coriander

⅛ teaspoon ground cinnamon

⅛ teaspoon turmeric

In a blender or food processor, process all the ingredients until creamy. Transfer to a small bowl and refrigerate until ready to use.

CHICKPEA FALAFEL

Serves 4

Chickpea patties, or falafel, are popular throughout the Middle East and North Africa, and are eaten as an appetizer, a snack, in a pita bread sandwich, or as a main dish.

1½ cups cooked or 1 (15.5-ounce) can chickpeas, drained and rinsed

½ cup chopped onion

1 garlic clove, chopped

¼ cup minced fresh parsley

2 teaspoons fresh lemon juice

¾ teaspoon ground cumin

½ teaspoon ground coriander

¼ teaspoon cayenne

½ teaspoon salt

¼ teaspoon freshly ground black pepper

¾ cup dried bread crumbs

Grapeseed oil, for frying

In a food processor, combine the chickpeas, onion, garlic, parsley, lemon juice, cumin, coriander, cayenne, salt, black pepper, and ¼ cup of the breadcrumbs, and process until well combined. Taste to adjust seasonings. Form the mixture into patties, using about 2 tablespoons of the mixture for each one. If the mixture is not firm enough to shape into patties, add another tablespoon or two of bread crumbs. Dredge the patties in the remaining bread crumbs. Heat a thin layer of grapeseed oil in a large skillet over medium-high heat. Add the patties and cook 3 to 4 minutes on each side, or until nicely browned. Repeat until all of the falafel are cooked.

NIGERIAN PEANUT SOUP

Serves 4

Peanuts and okra, used throughout Africa, are showcased in this spicy soup. If okra is unavailable, substitute sliced zucchini or cut green beans.

1 tablespoon grapeseed oil

1 yellow onion, chopped

1 carrot, chopped

1 red bell pepper, seeded and chopped

2 small fresh serrano or other hot chiles, chopped

½ cup creamy peanut butter

3 cups vegetable broth

1 (14.5-ounce) can diced tomatoes, drained

1½ cups cooked rice

½ teaspoon ground ginger

½ teaspoon ground coriander

1 cup fresh okra, cut into ¼-inch rings

Salt and freshly ground black pepper

½ cup roasted salted peanuts, crushed

Heat the oil in a large saucepan over medium heat. Add the onion, carrot, bell pepper, and chiles. Cover and cook until softened, about 10 minutes. Stir in the peanut butter, then add the broth, stirring to blend. Add the tomatoes and bring to a boil. Reduce the heat to low and simmer until vegetables are tender, about 15 minutes. Add the rice, ginger, and coriander, and simmer 10 minutes.

Use a stick blender to purée a portion of the soup or transfer 2 to 3 cups of the soup to a blender or food processor and purée until smooth, then return to the pot. Add the okra and season to taste with salt and pepper. Cook until the okra is tender, about 15 minutes longer. To serve, ladle the soup into bowls and sprinkle with the crushed peanuts.

WEST AFRICAN YAM AND GROUNDNUT STEW

Serves 4

Yams can sometimes be hard to find; however, they are generally interchangeable with sweet potatoes in recipes. In Africa, peanuts are known as groundnuts. For a less spicy stew, use mild chiles. Serve over rice or couscous.

2 tablespoons olive oil

1 yellow onion, chopped

3 garlic cloves, minced

1 red bell pepper, seeded and chopped

2 pounds sweet potatoes or yams, peeled and cut into ½-inch chunks

1 carrot, cut into ¼-inch slices

3 small fresh hot chiles, seeded and chopped

1 (14.5-ounce) can diced tomatoes, drained

⅓ cup peanut butter

3 cups vegetable broth

2 teaspoons light brown sugar, or a natural sweetener

½ teaspoon ground cumin

½ teaspoon ground coriander

½ teaspoon ground cinnamon

1 teaspoon salt

¼ teaspoon freshly ground black pepper

½ cup chopped or crushed roasted peanuts

Heat the oil in a large saucepan over medium heat. Add the onion, garlic, bell pepper, sweet potatoes, carrot, and chiles. Cover and cook, stirring occasionally, until the vegetables begin to soften, about 5 minutes. Add the tomatoes, peanut butter, broth, sugar, cumin, coriander, cinnamon, salt, and pepper, and bring to a boil. Reduce the heat to medium and simmer until the vegetables are tender and the sauce has thickened, about 30 minutes. Taste and adjust seasonings. Garnish with the peanuts and serve.

NORTH AFRICAN PUMPKIN STEW

Serves 4

Be sure to use the small pie pumpkin for this recipe, not the large jack-o'-lantern kind. You can also use a winter squash in this recipe, such as butternut or buttercup.

1 tablespoon grapeseed oil

1 large yellow onion, chopped

4 garlic cloves, finely minced

2 small, fresh hot chiles, seeded and chopped

1 teaspoon grated fresh ginger

½ teaspoon ground cinnamon

¼ teaspoon ground cumin

¼ teaspoon ground allspice

⅛ teaspoon ground cloves

2 pounds pumpkin or winter squash, seeded, peeled, and cut into ½-inch dice

1 (14.5-ounce) can diced tomatoes, drained

1½ cups water

1 tablespoon dark brown sugar, or a natural sweetener

Salt and freshly ground black pepper

1½ cups cooked or 1 (15.5-ounce) can dark red kidney beans, drained and rinsed

Heat the oil in a large saucepan over medium heat. Add the onion, cover, and cook until softened, about 5 minutes. Add the garlic, chiles, ginger, cinnamon, cumin, allspice, and cloves, and cook, stirring, for 1 to 2 minutes. Add the pumpkin and toss until evenly coated with the spices. Stir in the tomatoes, water, sugar, and salt and pepper to taste. Bring to a boil, then reduce the heat to low. Add the beans, cover, and simmer until the vegetables are tender, about 45 minutes.

SENEGALESE SOUP

Serves 4

This delicious West African soup is moderately spiced with curry and cayenne but balanced by the sweetness of apple and the creaminess of vegan yogurt. Add less cayenne if you want a milder soup. Additional garnishes might include chopped apple, raisins, or peanuts.

1 tablespoon grapeseed oil

1 yellow onion, chopped

2 celery ribs, chopped

2 teaspoons curry powder

2 Granny Smith apples, peeled, cored, and chopped

2 cups vegetable broth

1 cup apple juice

½ cup vegan yogurt

½ teaspoon cayenne

½ teaspoon salt

2 tablespoons minced parsley

Heat the oil in a large saucepan over medium heat. Add the onion and celery, cover, and cook until softened, stirring occasionally, about 5 minutes. Stir in the curry powder and apple and cook 2 minutes. Add the broth and apple juice and simmer for 10 minutes. Remove from the heat to cool slightly.

Transfer the mixture into a blender or food processor. Add the vegan yogurt, cayenne, and salt, and process until smooth.

Pour the soup into a large bowl and refrigerate for 2 hours or until cold. Serve chilled, garnished with the minced parsley.

MOROCCAN CHICKPEA AND LENTIL SOUP

Serves 4

Called harira in Arabic, this thick spicy bean and vegetable soup is eaten in Morocco to break the Islamic fast of Ramadan. While there are many versions of this soup in Morocco, chickpeas and lentils are usually included, making it a perfect beginning for a hearty vegan soup.

2 tablespoons olive oil

1 yellow onion, chopped

½ cup chopped celery

3 garlic cloves, chopped

1 (14.5-ounce) can diced tomatoes, undrained

¾ cup dried lentils

½ teaspoon ground cinnamon

½ teaspoon ground coriander

¼ teaspoon turmeric

¼ teaspoon ground ginger

¼ teaspoon ground cumin

¾ teaspoon salt

¼ teaspoon freshly ground black pepper

¼ teaspoon ground cardamom

1 tablespoon tomato paste

4 cups vegetable broth

1½ cups cooked or 1 (15.5-ounce) can chickpeas, drained and rinsed

2 teaspoons Harissa Sauce (page 115)

1 tablespoon fresh lemon juice

2 tablespoons chopped parsley or cilantro

Heat the oil in a large pot over medium heat. Add the onion, celery, and garlic. Cover and cook until softened, about 5 minutes. Add the tomatoes, lentils, cinnamon, coriander, turmeric, ginger, cumin, salt, pepper, and cardamom and cook 5 minutes longer. Stir in the tomato paste, then add the broth and bring to a boil. Reduce the heat to low, cover and cook for 45 minutes, or until the lentils are tender.

Add the chickpeas and harissa and cook uncovered for 10 minutes. Stir in the lemon juice and cook a minute longer. Serve sprinkled with the chopped parsley or cilantro.

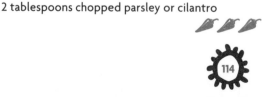

HARISSA SAUCE

Makes about 1 cup

The classic—and fiery—North African condiment is used in soups and stews or served with grilled vegetables. If you prefer more flavor than heat, use ancho or other mild chiles instead of hot ones.

8 to 10 dried hot red chiles
1 tablespoon olive oil
4 garlic cloves
1 teaspoon ground coriander
1 teaspoon ground caraway
½ teaspoon salt
2 teaspoons fresh lemon juice
¼ cup water

Stem and seed the chiles, and break them into pieces. Place the chiles in a heatproof bowl and cover with boiling water. Soak the chiles for 15 minutes. Drain but do not pat dry.

Combine the chiles, oil, garlic, coriander, caraway, and salt in a food processor and process to a paste. Add the lemon juice and water and process until smooth, adding a little extra water if the sauce is too thick. The sauce is now ready to use in recipes.

VEGETABLE TAGINE WITH SEITAN AND APRICOTS

Serves 4

A tagine is a boldly spiced Moroccan stew named after the earthenware pot in which it is traditionally cooked. It has a unique flavor that is at once sweet, sour, and spicy. If you omit the harissa, the dish will be nicely spiced without being hot. Instead of the seitan, you can use chickpeas or tempeh. Serve over freshly cooked rice or couscous.

1 cup dried apricots

1 tablespoon olive oil

8 ounces seitan, cut into ½-inch dice

1 yellow onion, chopped

2 carrots, chopped

1 red bell pepper, chopped

2 garlic cloves, minced

2 teaspoons minced fresh ginger

1 (14.5-ounce) can diced tomatoes, drained

½ teaspoon ground coriander

½ teaspoon cayenne

½ teaspoon salt

¼ teaspoon freshly ground black pepper

2 cups vegetable broth

1 teaspoon fresh lemon juice

1 teaspoon Harissa Sauce (page 115)

2 tablespoons minced fresh parsley

¼ cup toasted, slivered almonds

Soak the apricots in a bowl of hot water for 30 minutes, then drain, cut in half, and set aside.

Heat the oil in a large pot over medium heat. Add the seitan and cook until brown. Add the onion, carrots, bell pepper, garlic, and ginger. Cover, and cook until softened, about 5 minutes. Stir in the tomatoes, coriander, cayenne, salt, and pepper. Add the broth and bring to a boil. Reduce the heat to low and simmer for 30 minutes. Add the reserved apricots, lemon juice, and harissa, and cook 10 minutes longer. Stir in the parsley. Taste to adjust the seasonings before serving. Serve sprinkled with the almonds.

JOLLOF RICE AND BEANS

Serves 4

Many versions of Jollof rice exist throughout West Africa, where the rice and bean combination makes a satisfying and nourishing meal. Increase or decrease the amount of cayenne according to your own taste.

2 tablespoons grapeseed oil

1 yellow onion, chopped

1 green bell pepper, chopped

3 garlic cloves, minced

½ teaspoon cayenne

1 cup long-grain rice

1 (14.5-ounce) can diced tomatoes, drained

2 tablespoons tomato paste

2 cups vegetable broth

Salt and freshly ground black pepper

3 cups cooked or 2 (15.5-ounce) cans dark red kidney beans, drained and rinsed

2 tablespoons minced fresh parsley

Heat the oil in a large pot over medium heat. Add the onion, bell pepper, and garlic. Cover and cook until tender, about 5 minutes. Uncover and stir in the cayenne, then add the rice and cook, stirring for 1 minute.

Stir in the tomatoes, tomato paste, and vegetable broth. Season to taste with salt and pepper. Bring to a boil, then reduce the heat to low. Cover and cook until the rice is tender and the liquid is absorbed, 20 to 30 minutes.

Remove from the heat, stir in the beans, cover and set aside for 5 minutes. Taste to adjust seasonings. Serve garnished with the parsley.

ETHIOPIAN WAT

Serves 4

What's wat? It's Ethiopian for "stew," and it can be very hot and spicy, so take care when adding the seasonings. Ethiopian stews are made with a traditional spice mixture called berbere, which consists of chiles, garlic, coriander, ginger, and some hard-to-find spices. This adaptation comes close. It is traditionally eaten with injera, a spongy flatbread made with teff.

2 tablespoons olive oil

1 large yellow onion, chopped

3 garlic cloves, minced

1 teaspoon minced ginger

1 pound seitan, cut into 1-inch slices

½ to ¾ teaspoon cayenne

1 tablespoon tomato paste

½ teaspoon salt

½ teaspoon ground cumin

½ teaspoon ground allspice

½ teaspoon ground coriander

¼ teaspoon ground cardamom

1 (14.5-ounce) can crushed tomatoes

1 cup water

Freshly cooked rice

¼ cup ground or crushed roasted peanuts

Heat the oil in a large saucepan over medium heat. Add the onion, garlic, and ginger, and cook until softened, about 5 minutes. Add the seitan and cook, turning once, until lightly browned, about 10 minutes.

Add the cayenne, tomato paste, salt, cumin, allspice, coriander, cardamom, and tomatoes, and mix well. Stir in the water and bring to a boil. Reduce the heat to low and simmer for 30 minutes or until flavor has developed. Serve hot over rice, sprinkled with ground peanuts.

SPICY BLACK-EYED PEAS AND COLLARDS

Serves 4

The combination of black-eyed peas and collards is popular in the American South and can no doubt trace its roots to dishes such as this one from Africa. Serve over rice.

2 tablespoons olive oil

1 yellow onion, chopped

3 garlic cloves, minced

2 hot green chiles, seeded and minced

2 teaspoons grated ginger

8 ounces collard greens, coarsely chopped

2 cups water

1 teaspoon salt

3 cups cooked or 2 (15.5-ounce) can black-eyed peas, drained and rinsed

Freshly ground black pepper

Heat the oil in a large pot over medium heat. Add the onion, garlic, chiles, and ginger. Cover and cook until softened, about 5 minutes. Stir in the collards, water, and salt and bring to a boil, then reduce the heat to low and simmer until the collards are tender and most of the water is evaporated, about 20 minutes.

Stir in the black-eyed peas and pepper, to taste, and continue cooking until heated through. Taste to adjust seasonings.

AFRICAN YAM SALAD

Serves 4 to 6

Yams are indigenous to Africa, but the soft-fleshed orange sweet potatoes found in American supermarkets are often referred to as yams, to differentiate from the firm-fleshed yellow variety of sweet potatoes.

4 large sweet potatoes or yams

Salt

1 small red onion, minced

1 cup frozen peas, thawed

¼ cup grapeseed oil

3 tablespoons lemon juice

1 teaspoon sugar, or natural sweetener

¼ teaspoon cayenne

Place the unpeeled sweet potatoes in a saucepan and cover with water. Bring to a boil, salt the water, and cook until tender, but firm enough to slice. Cool and peel the sweet potatoes, cut them into ¼-inch-thick slices, and place them in a bowl. Add the onion and peas and set aside.

In a small bowl, combine the oil, lemon juice, sugar, and cayenne. Season to taste with salt and mix well, then pour over the potato mixture and toss gently to combine. Chill at least 1 hour before serving.

SPICY PEANUT TOMATO SALAD

Serves 4

If you've never tasted the combination of tomatoes and peanuts, you're in for a treat. Add more or less hot chile according to your taste.

4 ripe tomatoes, seeded and diced

3 scallions, chopped

1 small hot chile, seeded and minced

1 tablespoon chopped parsley

¼ cup peanut butter

3 tablespoons fresh lime juice

2 tablespoons olive oil

Salt

2 tablespoons crushed peanuts

In a bowl, combine the tomatoes, scallions, chile, and parsley. Set aside.

In a small bowl, combine the peanut butter, lime juice, oil, and salt to taste. Stir to mix well, then stir in 2 tablespoons of water, or more if needed, to make a smooth and pourable dressing. Add the dressing to the vegetables and toss to combine. Sprinkle with the crushed peanuts.

MARRAKECH COUSCOUS

Serves 4 to 6

This fragrant and colorful dish may be served hot, cold, or at room temperature. To amp up the protein, add a can of chickpeas.

2 cups vegetable broth or water

2 cups quick-cooking couscous

½ cup dried currants or raisins

2 tablespoons olive oil

2 shallots, minced

1 large red bell pepper, cut into ¼-inch dice

2 zucchini, chopped

1 carrot, shredded

1 hot chile, minced

4 scallions, minced

1 teaspoon ground coriander

½ teaspoon ground cumin

¼ teaspoon cayenne

¼ teaspoon turmeric

Salt and freshly ground black pepper

1 tablespoon fresh lemon juice

1 tablespoon minced fresh parsley

Bring the broth to a boil in a saucepan. Stir in the couscous and currants. Remove from the heat, cover, and set aside for 10 minutes.

Heat the oil in a large skillet over medium heat. Add the shallots, bell pepper, zucchini, carrot, chile, scallions, coriander, cumin, cayenne, turmeric, and season with salt and pepper to taste. Increase the heat to medium-high and cook until the vegetables begin to soften, stirring frequently, about 5 minutes. Add the reserved couscous mixture and the lemon juice, and cook until heated through, about 3 minutes. Remove from the heat and stir in the parsley. Taste to adjust seasonings.

EGYPTIAN FAVA BEANS

Serves 4

A traditional Egyptian breakfast of stewed fava beans, called ful medames, may sound a bit unusual to the uninitiated. But since it also makes a great high-protein lunch or dinner item, enjoy it whenever the mood strikes. If fava beans are unavailable, substitute lima beans. Add more cayenne for a hotter dish.

1 tablespoon olive oil

½ red onion, chopped

½ red bell pepper, chopped

2 garlic cloves, chopped

1 teaspoon ground cumin

⅛ teaspoon cayenne

2 cups cooked fresh, frozen, or canned fava beans, or limas

1 large ripe tomato, chopped

½ teaspoon salt

2 tablespoons chopped fresh parsley

Heat the oil in a saucepan over medium heat. Add the onion, bell pepper, garlic, cumin, and cayenne and cook 5 minutes, stirring. Add the cooked fava beans, tomato, salt, and enough water to simmer, about ½ cup. Cover, and cook about 10 minutes to heat through and blend flavors. Transfer the beans to a serving bowl and sprinkle with parsley.

MOROCCAN-SPICED CARROTS

Serves 4

The heady spices of Morocco make ordinary carrots extraordinary.

1 pound carrots, cut in ¼-inch julienne

Salt

1 tablespoon olive oil

1 teaspoon minced garlic

½ teaspoon ground coriander

½ teaspoon ground cumin

¼ teaspoon cayenne

¼ teaspoon ground cinnamon

2 tablespoons fresh lemon juice

1 tablespoon sugar, or a natural sweetener

2 tablespoons minced fresh parsley

Place the carrots in a saucepan, cover with water, add salt, and bring to a boil. Cook until the carrots are tender, about 7 minutes.

While the carrots are cooking, heat the oil in a small skillet over medium heat. Add the garlic, coriander, cumin, cayenne, cinnamon, lemon juice, sugar, and salt to taste, and stir until fragrant, about 2 minutes.

Drain the carrots and place in a serving bowl. Pour on the spice mixture, garnish with parsley, and serve.

SOUTH AFRICAN GREEN BEANS

Serves 4

The use of curry powder is indicative of the East Indian influence in South African cooking, but this dish is also delicious without the curry. Use your own curry spice blend or any good commercial brand.

1 pound green beans, trimmed

1 tablespoon grapeseed oil

1 yellow onion, chopped

1 garlic clove, mashed

1 fresh hot chile, minced

2 thin slices fresh ginger

½ teaspoon curry powder

Steam the green beans over boiling water until just tender. Run under cold water to stop the cooking process and retain the color. Set aside.

Heat the oil in a large skillet over medium heat. Add the onion and cook until browned, stirring occasionally, about 10 minutes. Add the garlic, chile, ginger, and curry powder. Mix well and add the green beans. Continue to cook over low heat, stirring occasionally, just until the beans are heated through and begin to brown, about 5 minutes.

WEST AFRICAN SPINACH WITH SPICY PEANUT SAUCE

Serves 4

Dishes flavored with peanuts and spiced with chiles are found throughout West Africa. This spinach dish is typical and delicious served over rice or couscous. Let your own heat tolerance be your guide on the amount of chiles to use. If you prefer, crumbled, dried chiles or hot red pepper flakes may be substituted for the fresh chiles.

1 pound fresh spinach, stemmed

1 tablespoon grapeseed oil

1 small yellow onion, chopped

2 garlic cloves, minced

2 fresh hot chiles, seeded and minced

1 (14.5-ounce) can diced tomatoes, drained and finely chopped

¼ cup creamy peanut butter

Salt

Steam the spinach over boiling water, until wilted, about 2 minutes. Remove from the heat and allow to cool. Chop the spinach and set aside.

Heat the oil in a large pot over medium heat. Add the onion, garlic, and chiles. Cover and cook until softened, about 7 minutes. Stir in the tomatoes and peanut butter and cook for 5 minutes, stirring to make a sauce. Add a little water if the mixture is too dry. Add the reserved spinach and cook, stirring, until hot. Season with salt to taste.

TUNISIAN COUSCOUS

Serves 4

A classic Tunisian couscous can be prepared in a couscoussière, but a regular saucepan will work just fine.

1 tablespoon grapeseed oil

1 yellow onion, cut into 1-inch dice

2 large carrots, cut into ½-inch slices

2 small turnips, peeled and quartered

1 red bell pepper, chopped

2 garlic cloves, chopped

3 cups vegetable broth

1 tablespoon soy sauce

¼ teaspoon turmeric

¼ teaspoon cayenne

Salt and freshly ground black pepper

1 (14.5-ounce) can diced tomatoes, drained

3 cups cooked or 2 (15.5-ounce) cans chickpeas, drained and rinsed

1 teaspoon Harissa Sauce (page 115)

1½ cups quick-cooking couscous

Heat the oil in a large pot over medium heat. Add the onion, carrots, turnips, bell pepper, and garlic. Cover and cook until softened, about 10 minutes. Stir in the vegetable broth, soy sauce, turmeric, cayenne, and salt and pepper to taste. Simmer uncovered until the vegetables are very tender, about 45 minutes. Stir in the tomatoes, chickpeas, and harissa, and keep warm over low heat.

In a saucepan, bring 2½ cups of salted water to a boil. Add the couscous, cover, and remove from the heat. Set aside for 10 minutes. To serve, spoon the hot couscous into shallow bowls and top with the vegetable mixture.

MOROCCAN RICE WITH APRICOTS AND PINE NUTS

Serves 4

This is a tasty way to use cold cooked rice, so plan ahead the next time you put on a pot of rice so you have plenty left over. Add additional spices to suit your taste.

½ cup dried apricots

1 tablespoon grapeseed oil

½ cup pine nuts or walnut pieces

3 scallions, minced

3½ cups cooked rice

2 tablespoons fresh minced parsley

½ teaspoon salt

½ teaspoon saffron threads or ground turmeric

¼ teaspoon cayenne

¼ teaspoon ground cardamom

¼ teaspoon ground cumin

Place the apricots in a heatproof bowl. Cover with boiling water and set aside to soften, about 30 minutes. Chop and set aside.

Heat the oil in a skillet over medium heat. Add the pine nuts, stirring for 2 minutes, or until lightly browned. Add the scallions, rice, reserved apricots, parsley, salt, saffron, cayenne, cardamom, and cumin. Cook, stirring until well mixed and heated through, about 10 minutes. Taste and adjust seasonings.

TOFU PIRIPIRI

Serves 4

Named for an incendiary red chile, in Africa the term piripiri has come to mean any dish that is spiced with hot red chiles. This fiery tofu dish certainly qualifies. Serve over rice or spear the tofu cubes with toothpicks and serve as an appetizer.

1 pound extra-firm tofu, drained and well pressed

3 garlic cloves, crushed

½ teaspoon ground cumin

½ teaspoon dried thyme

1 teaspoon cayenne

½ teaspoon salt

1 tablespoon fresh lemon juice

3 tablespoons olive oil

Cut the tofu into 1-inch cubes and place it in a shallow bowl. Set aside.

In a small bowl, combine the garlic, cumin, thyme, cayenne, salt, and lemon juice. Stir in the olive oil and mix well to blend. Pour the marinade over the tofu, tossing to coat. Cover and refrigerate for 2 to 3 hours.

Preheat the oven to 400°F. Transfer the tofu to an oiled baking pan, scraping any remaining marinade over the tofu. Bake until the tofu is golden brown, about 30 minutes.

CAMEROON-STYLE SEITAN AND SPINACH

Serves 4

This recipe is inspired by a dish called zom that is traditionally served with plantains or yams. Serve it over rice or couscous.

1 pound fresh spinach, stemmed

2 tablespoons grapeseed oil

8 ounces seitan, cut into 1-inch cubes

1 yellow onion, sliced

½ cup tomato sauce, commercial or homemade

1½ cups vegetable broth

2 tablespoons peanut butter

1 tablespoon soy sauce

¼ teaspoon cayenne

Steam the spinach over boiling water for 2 minutes. Remove from the heat, and allow to cool. Chop the spinach and set aside.

Heat 1 tablespoon of the oil in a large saucepan over medium heat. Add the seitan and brown on all sides. Remove the browned seitan with a slotted spoon and set aside.

Add the remaining 1 tablespoon oil to the saucepan. When hot, add the onion and cook until lightly brown, about 7 minutes, then reduce the heat and add the tomato sauce, broth, peanut butter, soy sauce, and cayenne. Cook, stirring occasionally, until the mixture comes to a boil, then lower the heat and simmer 10 minutes to blend the flavors. Uncover, add the reserved seitan and spinach and cook 5 minutes longer, or until hot. Taste to adjust seasonings before serving.

SEVEN VEGETABLE COUSCOUS

Serves 4

It is a Moroccan tradition to serve couscous with seven vegetables. The vegetables themselves can be varied, according to taste. The dish makes a pretty presentation with the couscous mounded in the center of a large platter surrounded by colorful vegetables.

2 tablespoons olive oil

1 yellow onion, chopped

2 garlic cloves, chopped

1 teaspoon ground cumin

1 teaspoon ground coriander

½ teaspoon ground cinnamon

½ teaspoon ground turmeric or saffron threads

¼ teaspoon cayenne

3 cups vegetable broth

1 sweet potato, peeled and cut into 1-inch chunks

2 carrots, cut into ½-inch slices

8 ounces green beans, cut into 2-inch lengths

1 pound small zucchini, halved lengthwise and cut into 2-inch pieces

1½ cups cooked or 1 (15.5-ounce) can chickpeas, drained and rinsed

1 (14.5-ounce) can diced tomatoes, drained

Salt

½ cup frozen peas, thawed

2 cups quick-cooking couscous

½ cup raisins

2 tablespoons minced parsley

Harissa Sauce (page 115)

Heat the oil in a pot over medium heat. Add the onion, garlic, cumin, coriander, cinnamon, turmeric, and cayenne. Cover and cook for 5 minutes. Stir in the broth, sweet potato, carrots, and green beans and bring to a boil. Reduce the heat to medium, cover, and simmer for 10 minutes. Add the zucchini, chickpeas, tomatoes, and salt to taste. Simmer another 10 minutes, until all the vegetables are tender. Stir in the peas and remove from the heat. In a saucepan, bring 2 cups of salted water to a boil. Add the couscous and raisins, cover, and remove from the heat. Let stand 10 minutes, then add the parsley and fluff with a fork. Mound the couscous in the center of a large platter and surround with the vegetables. Serve the Harissa Sauce on the side.

FOUR

India

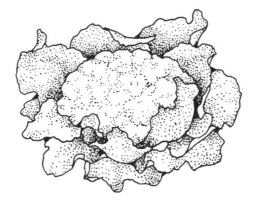

RECIPE GUIDE

THE FIERY BLISS OF INDIA

The vast subcontinent of India is home to some of the spiciest and most flavorful dishes in the world. This is mainly due to the use of curry, which is actually a blend of many spices. The prepared curry powder we find in Western grocery stores is unknown in India, and was developed out of the Western desire for convenience.

Curry mixtures achieve complex flavors because they are made with combinations of as many as twenty spices, including cumin, cardamom, cinnamon, ginger, turmeric, and cloves.

Curries are either made at home or ordered from shops. They are always spicy, but only hot if chiles are used.

Indian households make their own favorite masalas, or spice mixes, and specific combinations are used for particular dishes. A mixture of hot spices is called a garam masala, and I have included a recipe for a basic one in this book. However, if you don't want to mix your own spices, a trip to an Indian market would undoubtedly yield good-quality commercial products to your liking. In recipes calling for "curry powder,"

feel free to use a commercial blend or one you have mixed yourself. Curry spice mixtures are also available in the form of paste. It's fun to experiment with them until you find a favorite.

Rice and wheat are staples in India, as are lentils, kidney beans, chickpeas, split peas, and other beans that are used in the wide variety of meatless dishes enjoyed by the vegetarian Hindus of India. Generally, as in other countries, the hotter and spicier dishes are found in the southern regions, while milder and sweeter dishes are found in the north.

Indian cuisine includes a variety of delicious breads such as chapati and papadams. These breads help to absorb the fire of some of the more searingly hot dishes. Indian meals often include a creamy cucumber mixture called raita and a variety of chutneys and other condiments to help mellow the heat. Indian dinners usually end with a sweet pudding or fresh fruit, which can be a welcome respite after a particularly hot meal.

VEGETABLE PAKORAS

Serves 4

Pakoras, or fritters, are a popular appetizer in India. Vary the vegetables according to your preference.

½ cup unbleached all-purpose flour

½ teaspoon salt

¼ teaspoon cayenne

¼ teaspoon dried mint

2½ cups diced cooked cauliflower or potatoes

½ cup thawed frozen green peas

3 tablespoons grapeseed oil

Tamarind Dipping Sauce (page 164) or chutney, bottled or homemade

In a bowl, combine the flour, salt, cayenne, mint, and enough water to make a batter. Add the cauliflower and peas and mix well. Use your hands to shape into fritters and set aside.

Heat the oil in a large skillet over medium heat. Add the fritters in batches and fry until golden on both sides, turning once. Keep the cooked fritters warm in the oven until all fritters are cooked. Serve hot with tamarind sauce or chutney.

VEGETABLE SAMOSAS

Serves 4

A classic Indian appetizer, these vegetable-filled packets may also be made with packaged phyllo pastry or puff pasty dough. Although this dish is traditionally deep-fried, I prefer to use oil sparingly and finish the samosas in the oven.

2 cups unbleached all-purpose flour

4 tablespoons non-hydrogenated vegan margarine

½ teaspoon baking powder

Salt

½ to ¾ cup water

1 large russet potato, peeled and diced

1 carrot, chopped

3 tablespoons grapeseed oil

1 hot green chile, seeded and minced

½ teaspoon ground cumin

½ teaspoon curry powder or Garam Masala (page 163)

¼ teaspoon cayenne

¼ cup frozen peas, thawed

Tamarind Dipping Sauce (page 164) or chutney, bottled or homemade

In a bowl, combine the flour, margarine, and baking powder and ½ teaspoon of salt. Mix well. Add enough water to make a stiff dough. Knead until smooth and elastic. Steam the potato and carrot over boiling water until tender, about 10 minutes. Set aside.

Heat 1 tablespoon of the oil in a skillet over medium heat. Add the chile, cumin, curry powder, and cayenne. Stir in the potato, carrot, and peas, and season to taste with salt. Cook for about 5 minutes to blend the flavors. Set aside to cool.

Divide the dough into 2 pieces. Roll each piece into a rectangle and cut in half. Divide the potato mixture among each piece of dough, moisten the edges with water, and tightly seal.

Preheat the oven to 375°F. Heat the remaining 2 tablespoons of oil in a large skillet. Add the samosas and cook until golden. Transfer the samosas to a baking sheet and bake for 10 minutes or until heated through and browned. Drain and serve hot with tamarind sauce or chutney.

KASHMIRI VEGETABLE SOUP

Serves 4

The people of the mountainous region of Kashmir use spices grown in the Indian lowlands, such as cardamom, cinnamon, fennel, cloves, cumin, coriander, hot chiles, and turmeric. They love strong seasonings, and often do their cooking in a kerai, the Indian version of the wok. The chile adds the heat—without it, the soup is flavorful without being hot.

2 tablespoons grapeseed oil

1 teaspoon minced fresh ginger

1 teaspoon ground cardamom

½ teaspoon ground cumin

3 small Yukon Gold potatoes, peeled and quartered

2 small yellow onions, quartered

2 carrots, sliced diagonally into chunks

3 cups small cauliflower florets

1 small hot chile, seeded and minced

4 cups water or vegetable broth

1 teaspoon salt

¼ teaspoon freshly ground black pepper

1 ripe tomato, chopped

Heat the oil in a large pot over medium heat. Add the ginger, cardamom, and cumin and cook until fragrant, 30 seconds. Add the potatoes, onions, carrots, cauliflower, and chile. Cover and cook until slightly softened, about 5 minutes. Stir in the water, salt, and pepper and bring to a boil. Reduce the heat to medium, cover, and simmer until the vegetables are just tender, about 30 minutes. Stir in the tomato, taste to adjust seasonings, and cook 10 minutes longer.

MINT-FLECKED CURRIED POTATO SOUP

Serves 4 to 6

The natural sweetness of the mint brings out the flavor of the curry powder in this delicate creamy soup. The sweet potatoes give the soup a lovely orange blush. Add more or less curry powder (your own blend or a good commercial product) and cayenne according to your personal preference.

1 tablespoon grapeseed oil

1 small yellow onion, chopped

1 garlic clove, minced

2 teaspoons curry powder

⅛ teaspoon cayenne

4 cups water

1 pound russet potatoes, peeled and chopped

¾ pound sweet potatoes, peeled and chopped

1 teaspoon salt

1 cup soy milk

1 tablespoon minced fresh mint or ¼ teaspoon dried

Heat the oil in a large pot over medium heat. Add the onion and garlic. Cover and cook for 5 minutes. Stir in the curry powder and cayenne, and cook for 1 minute. Add the water, potatoes, sweet potatoes, and salt, and bring to a boil. Reduce the heat to medium, cover, and simmer until the vegetables are tender, about 30 minutes.

In a food processor or blender, purée the soup mixture in batches. Return to the pot, add the soy milk, and simmer over low heat. Taste and adjust seasonings, adding more salt if necessary. Ladle into bowls, sprinkle with the mint, and serve.

SPICY EGGPLANT AND POTATO STEW

Serves 4

Add some cooked chickpeas to this flavorful stew for additional texture and protein.

2 tablespoons olive oil

1 yellow onion, chopped

2 garlic cloves, minced

3 Yukon Gold potatoes, diced

1 eggplant, diced

1 hot green chile, seeded and minced

¼ teaspoon paprika

1 (28-ounce) can diced tomatoes, undrained

1 tablespoon curry powder

½ teaspoon coriander

½ teaspoon ground fennel seed

¼ teaspoon ground cumin

¼ teaspoon cayenne

2 cups water or vegetable broth

Salt and freshly ground black pepper

Heat the oil in a large pot over medium heat. Add the onion, garlic, potatoes, eggplant, and chile. Sprinkle the vegetables with paprika, cover, and cook for 5 minutes, or until the vegetables begin to soften. Reduce heat to low. Add the tomatoes and their juice, curry powder, coriander, fennel, cumin, cayenne, and water. Season with salt and pepper to taste. Cover and cook until the vegetables are tender, about 30 minutes.

CURRIED RICE SALAD

Serves 4

This colorful salad is ideal for casual buffets or potlucks because the flavor improves when the salad is allowed to stand at room temperature.

¼ cup grapeseed oil

⅓ cup mango chutney

¼ cup orange juice

2 tablespoons fresh lemon juice

1 tablespoon curry powder

¾ teaspoon salt

¼ teaspoon cayenne

2 large carrots, sliced thin on diagonal

½ cup chopped red bell pepper

1 hot chile, seeded and minced

2 scallions, minced

1 cup frozen peas, thawed and drained

3 cups cooked brown rice

2 tablespoons minced parsley

In a food processor, or bowl, blend the oil, chutney, orange juice, lemon juice, curry powder, salt, and cayenne until smooth. Set aside.

Steam the carrots over boiling water until just tender, about 3 minutes. Drain, rinse under cold water, and pat dry.

Transfer the carrots to a large bowl. Add the bell pepper, chile, scallions, peas, rice, and parsley. Pour on the reserved dressing and toss gently to combine well. Taste and adjust seasonings. Let the salad stand at room temperature for 15 minutes before serving.

SPICED POTATO SALAD

Serves 4 to 6

This Indian-spiced variation on potato salad raises an ordinary picnic food to exotic new heights. Cut back or eliminate the chiles for those who are less heat tolerant.

2 pounds small red-skinned potatoes

3 tablespoons grapeseed oil

1 yellow onion, chopped

3 garlic cloves

2 small fresh hot red chiles, cut into thin rings

2 teaspoons curry powder

½ teaspoon ground cumin

½ teaspoon ground coriander

½ teaspoon ground fennel seeds

¾ cup vegan yogurt

2 tablespoons minced fresh parsley

2 scallions, minced

1 tablespoon minced fresh cilantro

1 tablespoon minced fresh mint

½ teaspoon salt

¼ teaspoon sugar, or a natural sweetener

Place the potatoes in a saucepan with enough water to cover and boil until just tender, about 20 minutes. Drain, cut into bite-sized pieces, and set aside.

Heat the oil in a large skillet over medium-high heat. Add the onion, garlic, chiles, curry powder, cumin, coriander, and fennel. Cook, stirring, until the onions are softened but not browned, about 5 minutes. Add the potatoes and stir-fry until they are evenly coated with the seasonings and lightly browned, about 5 minutes. Transfer to a serving bowl and set aside.

In a food processor, combine the vegan yogurt, parsley, scallions, cilantro, mint, salt, and sugar, and process until well blended. Pour the dressing over the potatoes, and toss gently to combine. Chill for at least 1 hour before serving. Taste and adjust seasonings.

MANY BEAN SALAD

Serves 6

Don't be put off by the long list of ingredients. This attractive and delicious salad can be put together in minutes if you use canned beans or make the beans ahead of time and freeze them. If you don't have one of the beans on hand, double up on another, but strive for a variety, as that is the key to a colorful presentation. The finished dish looks especially nice in a large shallow bowl lined with curly endive or other salad greens.

¼ cup grapeseed oil

2 tablespoons cider vinegar

1 teaspoon sugar, or a natural sweetener

3 garlic cloves, finely minced

1 teaspoon minced fresh ginger

¼ teaspoon dry mustard

¼ teaspoon ground cumin

¼ teaspoon ground fennel seed

1½ cups cooked or 1 (15.5-ounce) can dark red kidney beans, drained and rinsed

1½ cups cooked or 1 (15.5-ounce) can chickpeas, drained and rinsed

1½ cups cooked or 1 (15.5-ounce) can black beans, drained and rinsed

1 cup thawed frozen peas

4 scallions, minced

¼ cup minced fresh parsley

1 tablespoon minced fresh cilantro

1 small fresh hot chile, minced

Salt and freshly ground black pepper

In a small bowl, combine the oil, vinegar, sugar, garlic, ginger, dry mustard, cumin, and fennel, and set aside.

In a large bowl, combine the kidney beans, chickpeas, black beans, and peas. Add the scallions, parsley, cilantro, and chile, and toss gently to combine. Pour the reserved dressing over the salad, season to taste with salt and pepper, and toss to combine. Let the salad marinate in the refrigerator for at least 1 hour before serving.

CURRIED MUSHROOMS

Serves 4

This creamy coconut curry sauce is also especially good combined with zucchini or cauliflower. Serve over freshly cooked basmati rice.

1 (13.5-ounce) can unsweetened coconut milk

1 teaspoon grated fresh ginger

3 garlic cloves, chopped

2 small fresh or dried chiles, seeded and chopped

1 teaspoon ground coriander

½ teaspoon ground cumin

½ teaspoon turmeric

2 tablespoons grapeseed oil

1 yellow onion, thinly sliced

1 pound white mushrooms, quartered

1 (14.5-ounce) can diced tomatoes, drained

Salt

In a blender, combine the coconut milk, ginger, garlic, chiles, coriander, cumin, and turmeric and blend until smooth.

In a large skillet, heat the oil over medium heat. Add the onion and cook, stirring, until golden brown, about 10 minutes. Add the mushrooms and cook until softened, 5 minutes. Stir in the tomatoes, the reserved coconut milk mixture, and salt to taste. Cook, stirring, until the sauce thickens, about 15 minutes.

QUICK RED BEAN DAL

Serves 4

One of the most basic Indian dishes, a dal can be a meal in itself or served as a companion to a curried dish. Dals can be made with a variety of different beans or legumes, such as lentils or peas, and can be quick and especially easy to prepare when made with canned beans. For a creamier texture, mash a portion of the dal with a stick blender.

3 cups cooked or 2 (15.5-ounce) cans dark red kidney beans, drained and rinsed

2 tablespoons grapeseed oil

1 yellow onion, chopped

2 garlic cloves, finely minced

1 tablespoon finely grated ginger

1 (14.5-ounce) can crushed tomatoes

2 teaspoons Garam Masala (see page 163) or curry powder

½ teaspoon ground coriander

¼ teaspoon cayenne

Salt

½ cup water

2 tablespoons chopped cilantro leaves

Place the kidney beans in a bowl and mash with a potato ricer. Set aside.

Heat the oil in a large saucepan over medium heat. Add the onion and garlic, cover, and cook until softened, about 7 minutes. Stir in the ginger, tomatoes, garam masala, coriander, cayenne, and salt to taste. Mix well. Add the reserved beans and water and simmer until the mixture is hot and the flavors are well blended, about 15 minutes, stirring frequently. Serve sprinkled with chopped cilantro.

SPICY INDIAN GREEN BEANS

Serves 6

Black mustard seeds are available at Indian markets and lend a distinctive flavor to this dish. However, if unavailable, simply omit them and the results will still be delicious.

1 pound green beans, cut in 1-inch lengths

2 tablespoons grapeseed oil

1 teaspoon black mustard seeds

1 yellow onion, chopped

1 small green hot chile, seeded and minced

1 teaspoon ground cumin

1 large ripe tomato, peeled, seeded, and chopped

¼ cup grated unsweetened coconut

1 tablespoon chopped fresh cilantro

2 tablespoons fresh lime juice

1 teaspoon sugar, or a natural sweetener

Salt and freshly ground black pepper

Cook the green beans in a large saucepan of boiling salted water until just tender, 5 to 7 minutes. Drain the beans, refresh them under cold water, and set aside.

Heat the oil in a large skillet over medium heat. Add the mustard seeds, and cook until they pop, about 30 seconds. Add the onion and chile and cook, stirring, until softened, about 5 minutes. Add the cumin and tomato and cook, stirring, for 2 minutes. Add the reserved green beans and cook, stirring, until the flavors are blended, about 5 minutes. Add the coconut, cilantro, lime juice, sugar, and salt and pepper to taste. Cook, stirring until hot and well combined.

SAAG

Serves 4

Saag is usually made with spinach or mustard greens. Indian restaurants often pair it with paneer, a type of cheese. Saag is especially good served with a warm Indian bread such as roti.

1 tablespoon grapeseed oil

1 garlic clove, minced

1 teaspoon grated fresh ginger

2 teaspoons hot curry powder or Garam Masala (page 163)

1 pound fresh spinach, stemmed and coarsely chopped

½ cup finely chopped tomatoes

Salt

Pinch cayenne (optional)

¼ cup unsweetened coconut milk (optional)

Heat the oil in a large skillet over medium heat. Add the garlic, ginger, and curry powder, and cook for 1 minute. Add the spinach, tomatoes, and salt to taste. Cook, stirring for 5 minutes to wilt the spinach. Simmer until the mixture is hot and the flavors are well blended, about 10 minutes. For extra heat add a little cayenne. For extra creaminess, pour in the optional coconut milk and simmer until well incorporated.

INDIAN-SPICED POTATOES AND CARROTS

Serves 4

The spices and the fruit juices bring out the natural sweetness of the carrots and potatoes.

1 pound Yukon Gold potatoes, peeled and cut into 1-inch dice

1 pound carrots, cut into ¼-inch slices

2 tablespoons grapeseed oil

2 garlic cloves, chopped

1 teaspoon Garam Masala (page 163)

½ teaspoon sugar, or a natural sweetener

¼ teaspoon ground cinnamon

¼ teaspoon ground cumin

⅛ teaspoon cayenne

¼ cup orange juice

1 tablespoon fresh lemon juice

Salt

2 tablespoons minced fresh parsley

Steam the potatoes and carrots over boiling water until just tender, about 8 minutes. Set aside.

Heat the oil in a skillet over medium heat. Add the garlic, garam masala, sugar, cinnamon, cumin, and cayenne and stir until fragrant, about 1 minute.

In a bowl, combine the reserved potatoes and carrots with the garlic mixture. Add the orange juice and lemon juice. Season with salt to taste and toss to combine. Serve at room temperature, garnished with parsley.

BRAISED CABBAGE WITH CARDAMOM

Serves 4 to 6

Cardamom is one of those distinctive spices that people either love or hate. Because it is expensive, make sure you like it before investing in a large quantity. If possible, buy a small amount of it, and any other spice you're not sure about, at a store where bulk spices are sold. Serve this dish over freshly cooked basmati rice.

2 tablespoons grapeseed oil

1 yellow onion, thinly sliced

2 garlic cloves, minced

1 tablespoon minced fresh ginger

1 head cabbage, chopped

1 teaspoon ground cardamom

½ teaspoon salt

¼ teaspoon ground turmeric

¼ teaspoon hot red pepper flakes

¼ teaspoon ground cinnamon

⅛ teaspoon freshly ground black pepper

1 cup water

Heat the oil in a large skillet over medium heat. Add the onion, garlic, and ginger, and cook until the onion is golden, stirring frequently, about 10 minutes. Add the cabbage, cardamom, salt, turmeric, red pepper flakes, cinnamon, and pepper, and cook, stirring, for 5 minutes. Stir in the water and bring to a boil. Reduce the heat to low, cover, and simmer about 20 minutes, or until tender. Taste to adjust seasonings.

GOBI MANCHURIAN

Serves 4

This exhilarating cauliflower dish comes to us from India via Chinese cooks who migrated there. The spicy, tangy sauce coats the succulent cauliflower florets for an unforgettable flavor combination. Serve it alone as an appetizer or atop freshly cooked rice as a main dish.

1 large head cauliflower, cut into medium florets

6 cloves garlic

2 teaspoons grated ginger

1¼ cups water, divided

½ cup all-purpose flour

½ cup cornstarch

1 teaspoon cayenne

Salt and freshly ground black pepper

2 tablespoons grapeseed oil

1 small yellow onion, chopped

3 Thai chiles, thinly sliced

½ cup ketchup

3 tablespoons soy sauce

1 tablespoon dark sesame oil

4 scallions, chopped

3 tablespoons coarsely chopped cilantro

Steam the cauliflower until just tender, about 5 minutes. Transfer to a bowl and set aside.

In a blender or food processor, combine the garlic, ginger, and ½ cup of the water and process to a paste. Remove about half of the garlic paste from the blender and transfer to a bowl. Set aside.

In the blender containing the remaining garlic paste, add the flour, cornstarch, cayenne, ½ teaspoon salt, ¼ teaspoon pepper, and a ½ cup of the water. Blend until smooth, adding a little more water, if needed, to make a smooth batter. Transfer the batter to a bowl.

Heat the oil in a large skillet over medium-high heat. Working in batches, dip the cauliflower in the batter and cook until golden, about 5 minutes. Use a slotted spoon to remove the cauliflower from the skillet and transfer to a plate.

Add the onion to the same skillet and cook for 5 minutes to soften. Add the chiles and the remaining garlic paste and cook, stirring for 2 to 3 minutes. Stir in the ketchup, soy sauce, sesame oil, and scallions. Add the remaining ¼ cup water and cook, stirring, for 1 to 2 minutes to thicken. Season with salt and pepper to taste. Toss the reserved cauliflower in the sauce, then transfer to a plate or shallow bowl and serve garnished with the cilantro.

ANSHU'S RED LENTIL SAMBAR

Serves 6

My friend Sangeeta Kumar has long raved about her Aunt Anshu's sambar, so I was thrilled when she gave me the recipe, which I have adapted here. Sambar powder is available in Indian markets and online. Serve over freshly cooked basmati rice.

1 cup red lentils

3½ cups water

2 tablespoons grapeseed oil

1 teaspoon black mustard seeds

1 onion, chopped

4 garlic cloves, minced

2 hot green chiles, seeded and minced

1 teaspoon grated ginger

1 (14.5-ounce) can diced tomatoes, drained

2½ teaspoons sambar powder

½ teaspoon ground coriander

¼ teaspoon cayenne

¼ teaspoon ground cumin

1 teaspoon salt

1 cup chopped carrots

1 cup chopped cauliflower

1 cup green beans, cut into 1-inch pieces

1 cup chopped eggplant

1 tablespoon fresh lemon juice

¼ cup chopped cilantro

Combine the lentils and water in a pot and bring to a boil. Reduce the heat to medium, cover, and simmer until soft, 30 minutes. Set aside, do not drain. Heat the oil in a skillet over medium heat. Add the mustard seeds. When they begin to pop, add the onion, garlic, chiles, and ginger and cook until softened, 5 minutes. Stir in the tomatoes, then add the sambar powder, coriander, cayenne, cumin, and salt. Add the carrots, cauliflower, green beans, and eggplant. Cover and cook for 5 minutes to soften. Add the vegetable mixture to the reserved lentils, cover, and simmer until the vegetables are soft, 20 minutes. If the mixture becomes too thick, add more water. Stir in the lemon juice and cilantro and cook 5 minutes longer. Taste and adjust the seasonings.

CURRIED NO-MEAT BALLS

Serves 4

Serve these little curried "no-meat balls" over basmati rice so you don't lose any of the flavorful sauce.

1½ cups cooked or 1 (15.5-ounce) can chickpeas, drained and rinsed

1 small yellow onion, chopped

¼ cup chopped peanuts

½ teaspoon minced fresh ginger

1 teaspoon minced fresh cilantro

2 teaspoons curry powder

¼ teaspoon cayenne

Salt

3 tablespoons grapeseed oil

2 garlic cloves, minced

1 teaspoon ground cinnamon

½ teaspoon ground cardamom

¼ teaspoon turmeric

½ teaspoon ground coriander

1 (14.5-ounce) can crushed tomatoes

1 cup vegan yogurt

1 teaspoon chopped fresh parsley

Place the chickpeas in a bowl and blot dry. Use a potato ricer to mash the chickpeas. Add about half of the chopped onion, the peanuts, ginger, cilantro, 1 teaspoon of the curry powder, ⅛ teaspoon of the cayenne, and salt to taste. Mix well, then shape into 1-inch balls. Heat 2 tablespoons of the oil in a large skillet and brown the balls on all sides. Remove from the skillet with a slotted spoon and drain on paper towels.

Heat the remaining 1 tablespoon oil in the same skillet. Add the remaining onion and brown lightly. Add the garlic, cinnamon, cardamom, turmeric, coriander, the remaining 1 teaspoon curry powder, the remaining ⅛ teaspoon cayenne, and salt to taste. Cook, stirring for 2 minutes, then stir in the tomatoes and simmer for 5 minutes, to blend the flavors. Remove the pan from the heat and whisk in the vegan yogurt. Carefully add the meatballs to the sauce, and warm over low heat without boiling. Serve garnished with the parsley.

CHICKPEA AND GREEN BEAN CURRY

Serves 4

Chickpeas and green beans combine in a tasty curry sauce for a hearty and healthful meal. For a hotter dish, use a hot curry spice blend or add more cayenne. Serve over rice.

2 tablespoons grapeseed oil

1 small onion, chopped

1 yellow or red bell pepper, chopped

2 garlic cloves, minced

1½ tablespoons curry powder

½ teaspoon ground cumin

½ teaspoon ground cinnamon

¼ teaspoon cayenne

½ cup water

1 pound green beans, cut into 2-inch lengths

Salt

1½ cups cooked or 1 (15.5-ounce) can chickpeas, drained and rinsed

½ cup soy milk or unsweetened coconut milk

1 tablespoon minced fresh cilantro

Heat the oil in a large skillet over medium heat. Add the onion, bell pepper, and garlic. Cover and cook until softened, about 5 minutes. Stir in the curry powder, cumin, cinnamon, and cayenne. Cook, stirring until fragrant, about 30 seconds. Add the water, green beans, and salt to taste. Cover, and cook until tender, about 8 minutes. Uncover, stir in the chickpeas, soy milk, and salt to taste, and simmer until hot, about 10 minutes. Taste to adjust seasonings, then transfer to a serving bowl, sprinkle with cilantro, and serve.

LENTILS IN ONION GRAVY

Serves 4

In this dal, hearty lentils are cooked in a gravy made rich and flavorful with onions, spices, and vegan yogurt.

1 tablespoon olive oil

1 large yellow onion, minced

2 garlic cloves, minced

1 teaspoon curry powder or Garam Masala (page 163)

½ teaspoon ground cardamom

½ teaspoon ground cinnamon

½ teaspoon ground cumin

¼ teaspoon cayenne

2½ cups water

1 cup red or brown lentils

1 teaspoon salt

½ cup plain vegan yogurt

Heat the oil in a large saucepan over medium heat. Add the onion and garlic, cover, and cook until softened, 5 minutes. Uncover, stir in the curry powder, cardamom, cinnamon, cumin, and cayenne, and cook 5 minutes longer, stirring to coat the onion and garlic with the spices. Stir in the water, lentils, and salt and bring to a boil. Reduce the heat to low, cover, and simmer until the lentils are tender and almost all the liquid has evaporated, 35 to 45 minutes, depending on the type of lentils used. Gradually stir in the vegan yogurt. Cook, stirring, until heated through, about 10 minutes. Taste and adjust the seasonings.

VINDALOO VEGETABLES

Serves 4

Serve this spicy vegetable mélange over freshly cooked basmati rice. Change the amount and type of vegetables according to personal preference and what's on hand. And, of course, you can tone down the heat by using fewer (or milder) chiles.

1 tablespoon grapeseed oil

1 yellow onion, chopped

3 garlic cloves, minced

1 tablespoon chopped fresh ginger

2 teaspoons Garam Masala (page 163) or a curry spice blend

1 teaspoon light brown sugar, or a natural sweetener

½ teaspoon paprika

2 carrots, thinly sliced

2 cups green beans, cut into 1-inch pieces

1 russet potato, peeled and diced

2 cups small cauliflower florets

1 green bell pepper, chopped

2 hot green chiles, seeded and minced

1 (14.5-ounce) can diced tomatoes, drained

1 tablespoon cider vinegar

1½ cups water

Salt and freshly ground black pepper

1½ cups cooked or 1 (15.5-ounce) can chickpeas, drained and rinsed

½ cup frozen green peas, thawed

Heat the oil in a pot over medium heat. Add the onion, garlic, ginger, garam masala, sugar, and paprika, and cook, stirring for 5 minutes. Add the carrots, green beans, potato, cauliflower, bell pepper, chiles, and tomatoes. Stir in the vinegar and water and season to taste with salt and pepper. Bring to a boil, then reduce the heat to medium, cover, and simmer until the vegetables are tender, about 20 minutes. Stir in the chickpeas and green peas. Taste and adjust the seasonings and cook 10 minutes longer to blend the flavors.

156

VEGETABLE MASALA

Serves 6

If fresh ripe tomatoes are not in season, use one 14.5-ounce can of drained diced tomatoes. This fragrant vegetable mélange should be served over freshly cooked basmati rice.

2 cups baby carrots

2 russet potatoes, peeled and cut into 1-inch chunks

1 tablespoon olive oil

1 yellow onion, chopped

3 garlic cloves, minced

2 teaspoons minced fresh ginger

1 red or green bell pepper, chopped

2 small zucchini, halved lengthwise, and cut into ¼-inch slices

1 (14.5-ounce) can diced tomatoes, drained

⅔ cup water

1 tablespoon Garam Masala (page 163)

1 teaspoon salt

Steam the carrots and potatoes over boiling water until just tender, about 15 minutes. Set aside.

Heat the oil in a large pot over medium heat. Add the onion, garlic, and ginger and cook, stirring, for 5 minutes to soften. Add the bell pepper, zucchini, tomatoes, and reserved carrots and potatoes. Stir in the water, garam masala, and salt. Cover and simmer until the vegetables are tender, about 15 minutes. Stir the vegetables, mashing some of the potatoes to create a sauce. Taste to adjust seasonings.

CASHEW PILAF
WITH RAISINS AND PEAS

Serves 4

Keep cooked rice on hand for this flavorful pilaf. It couldn't be easier or quicker to make, and it's versatile, too—you can add additional cooked vegetables or beans if you like.

1 tablespoon grapeseed oil

3 scallions, thinly sliced

3 cups cold cooked basmati rice

½ cup frozen peas, thawed

¼ cup golden raisins

1 tablespoon orange juice

1 teaspoon Garam Masala (page 163)

½ teaspoon salt

⅛ teaspoon cayenne

½ cup roasted cashew pieces

2 tablespoons minced fresh parsley

Heat the oil in a large skillet over medium heat. Add the scallions, rice, peas, raisins, orange juice, garam masala, salt, and cayenne, and stir to combine. Cover and cook until the rice is hot and the raisins are soft, about 10 minutes. Add the cashews and parsley and fluff with a fork to combine.

TANDOORI-INSPIRED VEGETABLES

Serves 4

These pungently spiced skewered vegetables are reminiscent of dishes made in a tandoor, a clay oven that cooks food at 900°F. This version is baked at 450°F, although you can instead cook them on a grill, if you prefer. If using wooden skewers, remember to soak them for 30 minutes before using to prevent them from burning.

1 cup plain unsweetened vegan yogurt

2 tablespoons grapeseed oil

1 tablespoon agave nectar

1 tablespoon ground coriander

2 teaspoons Garam Masala (page 163)

2 teaspoons finely grated fresh ginger

1 teaspoon minced garlic

1 teaspoon paprika

1 teaspoon salt

½ teaspoon ground cumin

½ teaspoon cayenne

½ teaspoon ground turmeric

3 to 4 large portobello mushroom caps, cut into 2-inch pieces

1 red bell pepper, cut into 1½-inch pieces

1 red onion, cut into 1½-inch pieces

8 cherry tomatoes

In a bowl, combine the yogurt, oil, agave, coriander, garam masala, ginger, garlic, paprika, salt, cumin, cayenne, and turmeric. Mix until well blended.

Add the mushrooms, bell pepper, onion, and tomatoes and toss to coat well.

Cover and refrigerate for 1 hour.

Preheat the oven to 450°F. Thread the vegetables onto skewers and arrange them in a single layer on baking sheets. Bake for 15 minutes. Turn the skewers carefully and continue to bake until the vegetables are tender, 10 to 15 minutes longer. Serve immediately.

GREEN TOMATO AND PEAR CHUTNEY

Makes about 3 cups

This zesty chutney is a great way to use up green tomatoes from the garden. In addition to making a delicious complement to Indian food, it's also great as a condiment for veggie burgers.

2 pounds firm green tomatoes, coarsely chopped

1 pound firm pears, peeled, cored, and chopped

1 cup light brown sugar, or a natural sweetener

1 cup apple cider vinegar

1 yellow onion, chopped

1 hot fresh or dried chile, chopped

½ cup golden raisins

¼ cup chopped crystallized ginger

1 tablespoon grated lemon zest

1 teaspoon ground allspice

½ teaspoon ground cinnamon

½ teaspoon salt

In a large saucepan, combine all the ingredients and bring to a boil, stirring occasionally. Reduce the heat to low and simmer until the mixture is very thick, stirring frequently toward the end of cooking time, about 1 hour.

Ladle the chutney into clean glass jars. Cool to room temperature, then cover tightly and refrigerate until ready to serve.

MINT CHUTNEY

Makes about 2 cups

This is one of my favorite chutneys because of its simplicity—there are very few ingredients, and no cooking is required. It's also a great way to use some of the mint that takes over my herb garden.

2½ cups fresh mint sprigs

4 scallions, chopped

1 hot chile, seeded and chopped

2 tablespoons fresh lemon juice

1 teaspoon sugar, or a natural sweetener

½ teaspoon salt

⅛ teaspoon ground cumin

2 tablespoons water

Combine all the ingredients in a blender or food processor. Process until smooth, adding more water if needed. Taste and adjust seasonings. Serve immediately or chill until ready to use.

PINEAPPLE DATE CHUTNEY

Makes about 2¹/₂ cups

The flavor of this chutney improves with time, so plan to make it several days ahead.

2 cups fresh or canned pineapple chunks

½ cup pitted and chopped dates

2 hot dried chiles, split lengthwise

½ cup light brown sugar, or a natural sweetener

2 tablespoons chopped crystallized ginger

¼ cup fresh lemon juice

½ teaspoon freshly ground black pepper

¼ teaspoon ground cloves

¼ teaspoon salt

Finely chop the pineapple and place it in a saucepan over medium heat. Add the dates, chiles, sugar, ginger, and lemon juice and cook until thickened, stirring occasionally, about 30 minutes. Remove from the heat and stir in the pepper, cloves, and salt. Transfer to a jar or container with a tight lid, allow to cool completely, then cover, and refrigerate.

GARAM MASALA

Makes about 1½ cups

Literally "hot mix," garam masala is a blend of spices, whose composition and ratio can vary greatly from cook to cook. An electric spice grinder is a good investment if you plan to grind a lot of your own spice mixtures. This will last for several months if you keep it tightly covered.

4 hot dried chiles
¼ cup whole cardamom pods
¼ cup whole black peppercorns
¼ cup cumin seeds
¼ cup whole cloves
⅛ cup coriander seeds
2 whole cinnamon sticks

Preheat the oven to 200°F. Spread out all the ingredients in a single layer on a shallow baking pan. Roast for 30 minutes, stirring occasionally. Remove the cardamom seeds and discard the pods. Break up the cinnamon sticks.

Place all the roasted ingredients in a blender or spice mill and pulverize at high speed until finely ground. Transfer to a container with a tight-fitting lid and shake to blend.

TAMARIND DIPPING SAUCE

Makes about 3/4 cup

Tamarind has a distinctively tart flavor. In this recipe, it is sweetened and spiced to produce a flavorful, ruby red sauce that is perfect for pakoras and samosas. Tamarind concentrate can be found at Indian grocery stores or online.

3 tablespoons tamarind concentrate

½ cup water

¼ cup light brown sugar, or a natural sweetener

1 teaspoon grated fresh ginger

¼ teaspoon cayenne

Combine all the ingredients in a saucepan and simmer over low heat, stirring occasionally, until thickened and syrupy, about 10 minutes. Cool before serving.

FIVE

Asia

RECIPE GUIDE

SEARING ASIAN APPETITES

Asian cooks have made many important contributions to the world's hot and spicy cuisines, particularly those from China, Korea, and Thailand. Most Asian cuisines use chiles as their source of heat along with a variety of other spices to create unique regional flavors. Japanese cuisine isn't especially spicy, but it's worth noting here for its use of the fiery green horseradish called wasabi, which is used as a condiment with sushi and sashimi. While meat and seafood are used throughout Asia, protein-rich vegan ingredients such as tofu, tempeh, and seitan (wheat gluten) are also used and easily substituted.

CHINA

The Sichuan and Hunan regions are home to China's most fiery dishes. Seasonings include garlic, ginger, soy sauce, and sherry, combined with hot red chiles in varying degrees. Rice and noodles are mainstays in the Chinese diet, and fresh vegetables include cabbage, bean sprouts, mushrooms, onions, and celery. Tofu, or bean curd, is a rich source of protein and provides a wonderful vehicle for the pungent Sichuan and Hunan sauces.

THAILAND AND SOUTHEAST ASIA

Perhaps some of the most incendiary dishes of all can be found in Southeastern Asia, particularly in Thailand. This is partly because of the liberal use of the Thai chile, one of the hottest chiles in the world. Because of its extreme heat, I don't specifically call for Thai chiles often in my recipes, as they can be difficult to find and too intense for many palates. Those who prefer slightly milder chiles can still enjoy the wonderful flavors of Thailand.

Thai food is a sensory marvel, bearing Chinese, Indonesian, and Indian influences that merge to create a distinctive cuisine in its own right. Many Thai dishes are prepared to present the subtle flavor variances of hot, sweet, sour, bitter, and salty, all at once.

Although Vietnamese food can be spicy, hot seasonings don't predominate. Tropical ingredients, such as the indigenous lemongrass and citrus fruits, are common and often accompanied by platters of bean sprouts, fresh herbs, cucumbers, and lettuce. A popular Southeast Asian seasoning is a fish sauce, called nuoc nam in Vietnamese and nam pla in Thai, that is used much in the way soy sauce is used in China. I have included a vegan version of "fish" sauce in this book.

KOREA

Korean cooking has been greatly influenced by the traditions of China, however it tends to be spicier than Chinese cuisine. A liberal use of chiles, soy sauce, garlic, and the ubiquitous kimchi (a searing fermented cabbage pickle) help to rank Korean cookery among the spiciest of Asian cuisines. A traditional Korean meal will include the colors green, white, yellow, red, and black, as well as a variety of textures and flavors. The typical Korean meal includes rice, soup, vegetables, a main course, and kimchi. Like most Asian cuisines, rice is an important mainstay, as is tofu, although Koreans also eat a variety of vegetables, along with barley, wheat, beans, meats, and fish.

INDONESIA

The Spice Islands of Indonesia were once the only place in the world where cloves and nutmeg grew. Though the cuisine of the islands of this archipelago is diverse, the most popular meals consist of rice with several savory side dishes, including a condiment called ketjap manis from which, it is believed, we derived our word "ketchup."

Indonesian cuisine has been influenced by the many cultures drawn to its spice treasures, foremost among them India, its neighbor just across the Bay of Bengal. However these are only influences. With its rich spices and indigenous herbs and produce such as lemongrass, coriander, and coconut, Indonesian cuisine is distinctive unto itself. When chiles, as well as ginger and garlic, are added to these ingredients, the results are full-flavored indeed. An especially interesting note for vegans: Tempeh—the popular meat alternative made from compressed soybeans—actually has its origins in Indonesia, where it is often prepared in coconut milk.

VEGETABLE SPRING ROLLS

Serves 12

These spring rolls are delicious, so make plenty. Serve with Spicy Peanut Sauce (page 199) or Hot Mustard Dipping Sauce (page 189). Be sure your spring roll wrappers are vegan—some brands may contain egg.

6 shiitake mushrooms, chopped

1 cup chopped bok choy

¼ cup bamboo shoots, chopped

¼ cup grated carrot

¼ teaspoon salt

⅛ teaspoon cayenne

1 tablespoon grapeseed oil, plus more for frying

1 tablespoon cornstarch

4 tablespoons cold water

12 vegan spring roll wrappers

1 tablespoon unbleached all-purpose flour

Combine the mushrooms, bok choy, bamboo shoots, carrots, salt, and cayenne in a bowl and let stand for 30 minutes. Heat 1 tablespoon of the grapeseed oil in a wok or skillet. Add the vegetable mixture and stir-fry for 2 minutes. Combine the cornstarch with 2 tablespoons of the cold water, add to the wok, and cook until thickened. Set aside to cool. Place a portion of the filling on the short end of each wrapper. Fold the top edge over. Fold in both ends and roll up lengthwise into a tight cylinder. Combine the flour with the remaining 2 tablespoons of cold water and use this paste to seal the ends. Heat the oil in a large saucepan until very hot. Fry the spring rolls, a few at a time, until golden brown, about 2 minutes. Drain on a paper towel.

GINGER WATERCRESS SOUP

Serves 4

The ginger and cayenne give this delicate, yet pungent, soup its bite. Sake, a fragrant Japanese rice wine, is a flavorful seasoning in many Asian dishes. Dark or toasted sesame oil has a rich, nutty flavor and is used as a seasoning, not for cooking, since it is not heat-stable at high temperatures.

8 ounces extra-firm tofu, cut into ½-inch dice

1 teaspoon plus 1 tablespoon grapeseed oil

¾ teaspoon cornstarch

¼ teaspoon cayenne

¼ teaspoon salt

4 cups vegetable broth

8 ounces watercress, stemmed

2 tablespoons soy sauce

2 teaspoons grated fresh ginger

1 teaspoon sake or dry white wine

1 teaspoon dark sesame oil

In a shallow bowl, combine the tofu with 1 teaspoon of the grapeseed oil, cornstarch, cayenne, and salt. Refrigerate for 1 hour.

Bring the broth to a boil in a saucepan. Add the watercress and soy sauce. Taste to adjust seasonings. Boil for 3 minutes, then reduce the heat to low and keep warm.

Heat the remaining 1 tablespoon of grapeseed oil in a skillet or wok over medium-high heat. Add the ginger and the reserved tofu and cook, stirring, for 2 minutes to blend flavors. Add the wine and sesame oil and cook for 1 minute, then transfer to the broth mixture. Cook for 3 minutes to blend the flavors. Serve hot.

FIVE-SPICE TOFU AND VEGETABLE SALAD

Serves 4 to 6

Five-spice powder is a blend of pungent spices used in Chinese cooking. It is available in Asian grocery stores, or you can make your own by combining the following ground spices: 1 teaspoon ginger with ¼ teaspoon each of allspice, anise, cinnamon, and cloves.

¼ pound snow peas, trimmed

3 tablespoons grapeseed oil

2 large garlic cloves, minced

1 teaspoon minced fresh ginger

1 pound extra-firm tofu, cut into ½-inch cubes

2 tablespoons rice vinegar

1 tablespoon sake, or dry white wine

1 teaspoon dark sesame oil

1 teaspoon hot chili oil

1 teaspoon sugar, or a natural sweetener

1 teaspoon salt

½ teaspoon five-spice powder

1 red bell pepper, cut into ½-inch dice

1 carrot, grated

4 scallions, chopped

½ cup dry-roasted cashews

Blanch the snow peas in boiling salted water for 1 minute. Drain and rinse under cold water, then pat dry and place them in a large bowl. Set aside.

Heat the grapeseed oil in a large skillet over medium-high heat. Add the garlic, ginger, and tofu and cook until the tofu is golden brown, about 5 minutes. Transfer the tofu to a plate, using a slotted spoon. To the skillet, add the vinegar, sake, sesame oil, chili oil, sugar, salt, and five-spice powder and bring to a boil, scraping up any browned bits. Remove from heat.

Add the bell pepper, carrots, and scallion to the bowl with the snow peas. Add the tofu and the sauce, and toss gently to combine. Cover and refrigerate at least 1 hour before serving. Just before serving, drain off the liquid and mix in the cashews. Taste to adjust seasonings.

COLD SICHUAN NOODLE SALAD

Serves 4

Some Chinese noodles contain eggs, so check the package carefully. Linguine makes a good substitute.

3 tablespoons rice vinegar

2 tablespoons soy sauce

1 tablespoon grated fresh ginger

2 tablespoons dark sesame oil

2 teaspoons sugar, or a natural sweetener

1 teaspoon hot chili paste

8 ounces egg-free Chinese noodles or linguine

1 red bell pepper, cut into ¼-inch strips

2 cups blanched broccoli florets

1 carrot, shredded

½ cup thinly sliced celery

4 scallions, minced

In a small bowl, combine the vinegar, soy sauce, ginger, sesame oil, sugar, and chili paste. Mix well, cover, and set aside at room temperature for 30 minutes.

Cook the noodles according to package directions. Drain the noodles immediately and rinse under cold water until cool. Drain again.

In a serving bowl, combine the noodles, bell pepper, broccoli, carrot, celery, and scallions. Add the reserved dressing and toss gently to combine. Cover and chill in the refrigerator until ready to serve.

SICHUAN CABBAGE

Serves 4

This spicy cabbage salad is similar to an Asian-style coleslaw.

3 carrots, shredded

4 cups shredded napa cabbage

¼ cup plus 2 tablespoons rice vinegar

1 tablespoon sugar, or a natural sweetener

2 tablespoons minced fresh ginger

2 teaspoons hot chili oil

2 teaspoons dark sesame oil

Steam the carrots and cabbage over boiling water until almost tender, about 3 minutes. Transfer to a large bowl and set aside to cool.

In a small saucepan, combine the vinegar, sugar, ginger, chili oil, and sesame oil. Bring just to a boil, stirring constantly. Reduce the heat to low and simmer 2 minutes. Set aside to cool completely. Pour the dressing over the vegetables and toss well to combine.

GINGER BROCCOLI

Serves 4

Although this recipe calls for broccoli, tofu will also work well, as will any favorite vegetable stir-fry combination. If you prefer your vegetables soft, cover the skillet with a lid during the cooking time to keep the steam in and hasten the cooking process.

2 tablespoons grapeseed oil

1 head broccoli, cut into 1-inch florets, stems reserved for another use

2 tablespoons soy sauce

1 teaspoon sugar, or a natural sweetener

1½ tablespoons grated ginger

1 scallion, chopped

1 garlic clove, minced

1 tablespoon dark sesame oil

1 teaspoon rice wine vinegar

¼ teaspoon hot red pepper flakes

Heat the grapeseed oil in a large skillet or wok over medium-high heat. Add the broccoli and stir-fry about 1 minute, or until bright green. Sprinkle the broccoli with the soy sauce and sugar. Add the ginger, scallion, and garlic and stir-fry 2 minutes. Stir in the sesame oil, vinegar, and red pepper flakes, and continue to stir-fry until the broccoli is crisp-tender, about 3 minutes.

FIVE-SPICE TEMPEH

Serves 4

Chinese five-spice powder is available in Asian markets and well-stocked supermarkets. It usually contains star anise, cloves, fennel, cinnamon, and Sichuan peppercorns.

1 pound tempeh, cut into 1-inch slices

1 tablespoon five-spice powder

¼ teaspoon cayenne

2 tablespoons grapeseed oil

Salt and freshly ground black pepper

1 cup vegetable broth

2 tablespoons grated orange zest

2 tablespoons sake, or dry white wine

1 tablespoon chopped fresh cilantro

Poach the tempeh in a pan of simmering water for 30 minutes. Pat the tempeh dry.

In a shallow bowl, combine the five-spice powder and the cayenne. Add the tempeh pieces, turning to coat with the spice mixture.

Heat the oil in a large skillet over medium heat. Add the tempeh and cook until browned on all sides, about 10 minutes total. Season to taste with salt and pepper. Keep warm.

Bring the broth to a boil in a saucepan and simmer until it is reduced by half. Add the orange zest and sake to the broth, and return to a simmer. Season with salt and pepper to taste. Pour the sauce over the reserved tempeh. Serve sprinkled with the cilantro.

ASIAN FUSION NOODLES

Serves 4

In the true spirit of a fusion dish, this Asian-style stir-fry is made with spaghetti, but your favorite noodles may be used instead. This is a good recipe for adding extra embellishments that you may have on hand or that appeal to you, such as baby corn, straw mushrooms, lotus root, and so on.

12 ounces spaghetti

1 tablespoon dark sesame oil

1 tablespoon grapeseed oil

3 garlic cloves, minced

1 tablespoon minced fresh ginger

1 red bell pepper, cut into thin strips

2 cups chopped napa cabbage

2 scallions, chopped

1½ tablespoons sesame paste

1 tablespoon hot chili oil

2 tablespoons soy sauce

1 cup vegetable broth

½ cup walnut pieces

Cook the spaghetti in a pot of boiling salted water until tender, about 10 minutes. Drain and place in a large bowl. Drizzle on the sesame oil and toss to combine. Set aside.

In a large skillet or wok, heat the grapeseed oil over medium-high heat. Add the garlic, ginger, bell pepper, cabbage, and scallions and stir-fry until softened, 3 minutes. Remove from the heat and set aside.

In a small bowl, combine the sesame paste, chili oil, soy sauce, and about half the vegetable broth, stirring to blend. Return the skillet to the heat, add the reserved spaghetti, pour on the sauce, and add the walnuts. Stir-fry until the noodles are hot and coated with sauce, adding more of the remaining broth, if needed.

STIR-FRIED GINGER SEITAN AND BOK CHOY

Serves 4

With its pale ribs and dark green leaves, bok choy, or Chinese cabbage, looks like a cross between celery and Swiss chard. It is a common ingredient in Chinese stir-fries and has a more subtle flavor than head cabbage. As with most stir-fries, this is best served over rice.

2 tablespoons grapeseed oil

8 ounces seitan, cut into ½ by 2-inch strips

4 garlic cloves, minced

1 tablespoon minced fresh ginger

1 yellow onion, sliced thin

2 small thin, fresh hot chiles, seeded and halved

2 tablespoons soy sauce

2 tablespoons water

¼ teaspoon five-spice powder

¼ teaspoon freshly ground black pepper

½ teaspoon sugar, or a natural sweetener

1 tablespoon dry sherry

1 pound bok choy, cut crosswise into ½-inch strips

Heat the oil in a large skillet or wok over medium-high heat. Add the seitan and stir-fry until browned all over. Remove the seitan from the skillet and set aside.

To the same skillet, add the garlic and ginger and stir-fry for 30 seconds. Add the onion and chiles and stir-fry for 3 minutes. Add the soy sauce, water, five-spice powder, pepper, sugar, and sherry, and toss together. Add the bok choy to the pan and stir-fry until the greens are wilted. Return the seitan to the pan, and cook, stirring until hot.

SICHUAN VEGETABLES

Serves 4

Shiitake mushrooms are among the few mushrooms that grow on logs instead of in soil. Aromatic and chewy with a subtly woodsy flavor, shiitakes absorb the taste of the ingredients with which they are cooked. Once only commonly found in the dried form, they are now available fresh in most supermarkets.

1 tablespoon grapeseed oil

1 tablespoon grated fresh ginger

2 scallions, minced

2 garlic cloves, minced

2 small hot red chiles, split lengthwise

½ cup grated carrots

½ cup chopped red bell pepper

1 cup thinly sliced fresh shiitake mushroom caps

2 cups thinly sliced napa cabbage

3 tablespoons dry sherry

2 tablespoons soy sauce

2 tablespoons dark sesame oil

1 teaspoon sugar, or a natural sweetener

Heat the grapeseed oil in a large skillet or wok over medium-high heat. Add the ginger, scallions, garlic, and chiles, and stir-fry for 1 minute. Add the carrots, bell pepper, mushrooms, and cabbage and stir-fry 3 to 5 minutes or until vegetables soften.

In a small bowl, combine the sherry, soy sauce, sesame oil, and sugar. Add to the vegetables and stir to coat.

SLIVERED SEITAN AND VEGETABLE STIR-FRY

Serves 4

One of the excellent Chinese beers such as Tsingtao will help put out the fire of this tantalizing stir-fry. Serve over rice.

⅓ cup water

3 tablespoons rice vinegar

2 tablespoons light brown sugar, or a natural sweetener

¼ cup soy sauce

1½ teaspoons tomato paste

2 tablespoons minced garlic

1 tablespoon grated fresh ginger

½ teaspoon dry mustard

½ teaspoon hot red pepper flakes

2 tablespoons hoisin sauce

1 teaspoon cornstarch dissolved in 1 tablespoon water

2 tablespoons grapeseed oil

1 yellow onion, thinly sliced

1 green bell pepper, cut into thin strips

1 red bell pepper, cut into thin strips

8 ounces broccoli florets, blanched

8 ounces seitan, cut into thin slivers

½ cup canned water chestnuts, drained and rinsed

In a saucepan, combine the water, vinegar, sugar, soy sauce, tomato paste, garlic, ginger, mustard, hot red pepper flakes, and hoisin sauce, and bring to a boil, stirring until well mixed. Reduce the heat to medium and simmer for 10 minutes, stirring occasionally to prevent sticking. Stir in the cornstarch mixture and simmer until the sauce is thickened and translucent. Set aside.

In a large skillet or wok, heat the oil over medium-high heat. Add the onion and bell peppers, and stir-fry for about 2 minutes. Add the broccoli and stir-fry until crisp tender, about 3 minutes. Add the seitan and water chestnuts, and stir-fry until the seitan is browned, about 5 minutes longer. Stir in the sauce and stir-fry until the seitan and vegetables are coated.

179

HUNAN VEGETABLE STIR-FRY

Serves 4

This versatile stir-fry can be made using different vegetables or with the addition of tofu or seitan for a main dish. For a mild yet flavorful version, omit the hot red pepper flakes and red wine vinegar.

½ teaspoon hot red pepper flakes

1½ teaspoons red wine vinegar

½ cup tomato purée

¼ cup dry sherry

¼ cup soy sauce

1 tablespoon dark sesame oil

1 tablespoon sugar, or a natural sweetener

2 tablespoons grapeseed oil

1 tablespoon grated fresh ginger

3 garlic cloves, minced

1 pound bok choy, thinly sliced

1 large carrot, shredded

4 ounces snow peas, trimmed

8 ounces mushrooms, sliced

Soak the red pepper flakes in the wine vinegar in a small bowl for 30 minutes.

In another small bowl, combine the tomato purée, sherry, soy sauce, sesame oil, and sugar, and set aside.

Heat the grapeseed oil in a large skillet or wok over medium-high heat. Add the ginger, garlic, bok choy, carrot, and undrained red pepper flakes, and stir-fry for 2 minutes. Add the snow peas and mushrooms and stir-fry for 3 minutes longer. Add the reserved sauce and cook until heated through.

SEITAN IN SPICY ORANGE SAUCE

Serves 4

This dish is reminiscent of the orange beef dish popular in American Chinese restaurants. For a complete meal, add some blanched asparagus or broccoli to the stir-fry and serve over rice.

2 tablespoons grapeseed oil

12 ounces seitan, cut into ½-inch strips

1 teaspoon minced garlic

1 teaspoon grated ginger

2 tablespoons soy sauce

2 tablespoons light brown sugar, or a natural sweetener

1 tablespoon rice vinegar

1½ teaspoons Asian chili paste

2 tablespoons orange zest

1 cup orange juice

1 tablespoon cornstarch dissolved in 2 tablespoons cold water

Heat 1 tablespoon of the oil in a large skillet or wok over medium-high heat. Add the seitan and stir-fry until browned, about 5 minutes. Remove from the skillet and set aside.

Heat the remaining oil in the same skillet over medium heat. Add the garlic and ginger and cook for 30 seconds. Stir in the soy sauce, brown sugar, rice vinegar, chili paste, and orange zest. Add the orange juice and bring to a boil. Stir in the cornstarch mixture and cook, stirring until the sauce thickens. Remove from heat and return the seitan to the skillet, tossing to coat with the sauce.

RED HOT CHILE TOFU

Serves 4

Hot chili paste is available in Asian markets and well-stocked supermarkets. Add more or less according to your heat tolerance. The tomato paste and chili paste combine to turn the tofu a lovely red color. Serve over rice with steamed or stir-fried vegetables.

2 tablespoons tomato paste

1 tablespoon water

1 tablespoon soy sauce

2 teaspoons sake, or dry white wine

¾ teaspoon sugar, or a natural sweetener

¼ cup cornstarch

½ teaspoon salt

1 pound extra-firm tofu, drained and cut into ½-inch strips

3 tablespoons grapeseed oil

¼ cup minced scallions

1 teaspoon minced garlic

1 teaspoon minced fresh ginger

1 teaspoon hot chili paste

In a small bowl, combine the tomato paste, water, soy sauce, sake, and sugar. Mix well and set aside.

In a shallow bowl, combine the cornstarch and salt. Dredge the tofu strips in the cornstarch mixture, shaking off any excess.

Heat 2 tablespoons of the oil in a large skillet or wok over medium-high heat. Add the tofu in batches and cook until golden brown. Transfer to a platter.

Heat the remaining 1 tablespoon of oil in the same skillet or wok over medium-high heat. Add the scallions, garlic, ginger, and chili paste, and cook, stirring for 15 seconds. Add the reserved tomato paste mixture and stir until well blended. Add the reserved tofu and toss gently to coat with the sauce, cooking until heated through, about 3 minutes.

THREE-ALARM LO MEIN

Serves 4

Lo mein is typically mild, but we like to spice it up at our house with some hot chili oil. If egg-free Chinese noodles are unavailable, substitute linguine for this hearty one-dish meal. Baked marinated tofu is available in well-stocked supermarkets and natural food stores. If unavailable, use regular extra-firm tofu.

2 tablespoons dry sherry

1 teaspoon cornstarch

12 ounces egg-free Chinese noodles or linguine

2 teaspoons dark sesame oil

1 tablespoon hot chili oil

2 tablespoons grapeseed oil

1 small head bok choy, trimmed and cut into ¼-inch slices

6 scallions, thinly sliced

1 tablespoon minced fresh ginger

6 shiitake mushrooms, trimmed and sliced

3 tablespoons soy sauce

2 tablespoons water

1 tablespoon hoisin sauce

8 ounces Asian-flavored baked marinated tofu, cut into ½-inch dice

In a shallow bowl, combine the sherry with the cornstarch, and mix until well blended. Set aside.

Cook the noodles in a large pot of boiling water until tender. Drain, rinse under cold water, and drain again. Transfer to a bowl, add the sesame oil and chili oil, and toss to combine.

Heat the grapeseed oil in a large skillet or wok over medium-high heat. Add the bok choy, scallions, ginger, and mushrooms and stir-fry for 2 minutes. Add the soy sauce, water, hoisin, and reserved sherry mixture and stir-fry for 3 minutes. Add the reserved noodles and the tofu and stir-fry until hot.

HUNAN FRIED RICE
Serves 4

This is a flavorful, slightly hot, version of fried rice from the Hunan region of China, which is known for its spicy dishes. It tastes like restaurant-style fried rice but without the MSG and extra oil. Omit the red pepper flakes for a mild version.

3 tablespoons soy sauce

2 tablespoons dry sherry

1 tablespoon dark sesame oil

1 tablespoon light brown sugar,
or a natural sweetener

1 teaspoon grated fresh ginger

1 garlic clove, minced

1 teaspoon Sriracha sauce

1 pound extra-firm tofu, drained and cut
into ½-inch dice

2 teaspoons cornstarch

2 tablespoons grapeseed oil

1 red bell pepper, chopped

1 cup shredded cabbage

¼ cup minced scallions

½ teaspoon red pepper flakes

3 cups cold cooked rice

In a shallow bowl, combine the soy sauce, sherry, sesame oil, brown sugar, ginger, garlic, and Sriracha. Add the tofu and refrigerate for 30 minutes.

Drain the tofu, reserving the marinade. Blend the reserved marinade with the cornstarch and add to the tofu, tossing to coat.

Heat the grapeseed oil in a large skillet or wok over medium-high heat. Add the bell pepper, cabbage, scallions, and red pepper flakes, and stir-fry 2 minutes. Add the tofu and marinade and stir-fry until the liquid is nearly absorbed. Add the rice and stir-fry until heated through and well combined.

TOFU AND BROCCOLI WITH HOISIN-GINGER SAUCE

Serves 4

Hoisin sauce is a fragrant, spicy-sweet sauce that can be used to add flavor to a variety of Chinese dishes. It is available in well-stocked supermarkets. If you want all the flavor without the heat, omit the red pepper flakes. Serve over rice.

2 cups broccoli florets

⅓ cup hoisin sauce

1 teaspoon Asian chili paste

2 tablespoons soy sauce

2 tablespoons water

1 tablespoon grapeseed oil

1 pound extra-firm tofu, drained, blotted, and cut into 1-inch dice

1 tablespoon minced fresh ginger

¼ cup minced scallions

Steam the broccoli until just tender. Run under cold water to stop the cooking process, and set aside.

In a small bowl, combine the hoisin, chili paste, soy sauce, and water and set aside.

Heat the oil in a large skillet or wok over medium heat. Add the tofu and cook until golden brown, about 10 minutes. Add the ginger and scallions and stir-fry for about 30 seconds. Stir in the hoisin mixture and cook, stirring, until the sauce thickens and the flavors have had a chance to blend, about 5 minutes. Add the reserved broccoli and cook until hot, stirring to coat.

BAKED MAHOGANY TEMPEH

Serves 4

The flavorful marinade gives the tempeh a rich mahogany color and wonderful flavor. Only mildly spicy as is, you can amp up the heat, if you wish, by adding more cayenne or some Asian chili paste to the marinade.

1 pound tempeh, cut into 2-inch bars

¼ cup soy sauce

2 tablespoons mirin

2 tablespoons agave nectar or brown rice syrup

2 garlic cloves

2 teaspoons chopped fresh ginger

¼ teaspoon ground coriander

¼ teaspoon cayenne

Grated zest of 1 orange

Poach the tempeh in simmering water for 30 minutes. Place the tempeh in a shallow baking dish and set aside.

In a bowl, combine the soy sauce, mirin, agave nectar, garlic, ginger, coriander, cayenne, and orange zest, and mix well. Pour the marinade over the tempeh and marinate at room temperature, basting often, for 30 minutes to an hour.

Preheat the oven to 425°F. Bake the tempeh, basting often with the marinade, until golden brown, 20 to 30 minutes.

SPICY TOFU AND ASPARAGUS STIR-FRY

Serves 4

I prefer using pencil-thin asparagus for this stir-fry, because it cooks quickly and doesn't require paring. If all you have are thick spears, be sure to pare them, especially near the bottom.

2 tablespoons soy sauce

1 tablespoon dark sesame oil

1 tablespoon water

2 teaspoons cornstarch

1 teaspoon sugar, or a natural sweetener

1 tablespoon grapeseed oil

1 pound asparagus, cut diagonally into 2-inch pieces

8 ounces extra-firm tofu, drained and cut into ½-inch cubes

2 garlic cloves, minced

1 tablespoon minced fresh ginger

2 scallions, minced

½ teaspoon hot red pepper flakes

In a small bowl, stir together the soy sauce, sesame oil, water, cornstarch, and sugar. Set aside.

In a large skillet or wok, heat the grapeseed oil over medium-high heat. Add the asparagus and stir-fry for 2 minutes, transferring the cooked asparagus to a bowl using a slotted spoon.

In the same skillet, add the tofu, garlic, ginger, scallions, and red pepper flakes, and stir-fry until the tofu is golden brown, about 5 minutes. Return the asparagus to the skillet and stir-fry for 1 minute. Add the soy sauce mixture and stir-fry 1 minute longer, or until hot.

SPICY SICHUAN SAUCE

Makes about 1/2 cup

Use this sauce as a dipping sauce for fried tofu or add it to your next stir-fry to wake up your taste buds.

2 teaspoons grapeseed oil

1 teaspoon minced garlic

1 teaspoon minced fresh ginger

1 tablespoon minced scallion

½ teaspoon hot red pepper flakes

1 tablespoon soy sauce

1 tablespoon light brown sugar, or a natural sweetener

1 tablespoon water

1 teaspoon rice vinegar

1 tablespoon dark sesame oil

Heat the grapeseed oil in a small saucepan over medium heat. Add the garlic, ginger, scallion, and red pepper flakes, and cook for 2 minutes. Stir in the soy sauce, brown sugar, water, and vinegar, and cook for 1 minute. Strain the sauce into a small bowl and stir in the sesame oil.

HOT MUSTARD DIPPING SAUCE

Makes about ½ cup

This sauce can be made a day ahead of time if covered tightly and refrigerated. Serve with spring rolls or tempura vegetables.

1 tablespoon light brown sugar

1 tablespoon dry mustard

3 tablespoons soy sauce

3 tablespoons water

1 tablespoon rice vinegar

Combine all the ingredients in a small saucepan, stirring to blend. Bring to a boil, then reduce the heat to low and cook for 1 minute to blend the flavors. Set aside to cool, then transfer to a small container, cover, and refrigerate until ready to use.

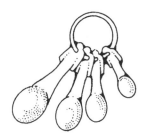

CHILE-KISSED CORN AND GINGER SOUP

Serves 4 to 6

The natural sweetness of the corn is complemented by the fragrant ginger and cilantro. A swirl of chili paste added just prior to serving will give the soup a touch of heat.

2 tablespoons grapeseed oil

½ cup chopped yellow onion

1 tablespoon minced fresh ginger

3 cups fresh or frozen corn kernels

3 cups vegetable broth

1 cup soy milk or unsweetened coconut milk

2 teaspoons minced fresh lemongrass, white part only, or zest of 1 lemon

2 teaspoons light brown sugar, or a natural sweetener

Salt and freshly ground black pepper

2 teaspoons hot chili paste

2 tablespoons minced fresh cilantro

Heat the oil in a saucepan over low heat. Add the onion and ginger and cook, stirring for 5 minutes. Stir in the corn, then add the broth and simmer until the corn is tender, about 5 minutes. Add the soy milk, lemongrass, and sugar. Season with salt and pepper, to taste. Cool completely.

Purée the soup (in batches if necessary) in a blender or food processor. Return to the saucepan and bring to a simmer. Transfer the soup to bowls and swirl ½ teaspoon chili paste into the center of each serving. Garnish with cilantro. Serve immediately.

SPICY PUMPKIN SOUP
Serves 4 to 6

This creamy, spicy soup is flavored with ginger, lime, lemongrass, and cilantro. Lemongrass is a pungent lemony stalk often found in Thai and Vietnamese cooking, although if you are unable to find it, you can substitute lemon zest. The flavor of the soup improves when reheated several hours after it is made.

1 tablespoon grapeseed oil

1 small yellow onion, chopped

1 tablespoon chopped fresh ginger

3 hot dried Thai chiles, split lengthwise, or ½ teaspoon hot red pepper flakes

2 teaspoons minced fresh lemongrass, white part only, or zest of 1 lemon

3 cups vegetable broth

3 tablespoons soy sauce

1 (16-ounce) can solid-pack pumpkin

1 (13.5-ounce) can unsweetened coconut milk

⅓ cup creamy peanut butter

1 tablespoon light brown sugar, or a natural sweetener

Salt

2 tablespoons fresh lime juice

¼ cup chopped fresh cilantro or Thai basil

2 tablespoons crushed roasted peanuts

Heat the oil in a pot over medium heat. Add the onion, ginger, and chiles and cook until softened, about 3 minutes. Stir in the lemongrass, broth, and soy sauce and bring to a boil, then reduce the heat to medium and simmer for 10 minutes.

Strain the broth into another pot, discard the solids and place the pot on the stove over low heat. Whisk in the pumpkin, coconut milk, peanut butter, and sugar and season to taste with salt. Cook, stirring, until smooth and hot, about 10 minutes. Do not boil. Stir in the lime juice, taste, and adjust the seasonings. Serve hot, garnished with cilantro and peanuts.

HOT AND SOUR THAI SOUP

Serves 4

The popular Thai soup called tom yum is known for its flavorful broth spiced with chiles and lemongrass. Lemon zest can be used to replace lemongrass in this and other recipes.

5 cups vegetable broth

2 (1-inch) pieces lemongrass, white part only, crushed, or zest of 1 lemon

1 garlic clove, crushed

4 dried Thai or other hot chiles, split lengthwise

½ red bell pepper, cut into thin strips

1 cup sliced mushrooms

3 scallions, chopped

8 ounces extra-firm tofu, cut into ½-inch dice

2 tablespoons Vegan "Fish" Sauce (page 220) or soy sauce

1 tablespoon fresh lime juice

¼ cup fresh cilantro, coarsely chopped

In a saucepan, combine the broth, lemongrass, garlic, and chiles. Bring to a boil, cover, reduce the heat, and simmer for 30 minutes. Strain the mixture through a sieve, discard the solids, and return the liquid to a saucepan. Add the bell pepper, mushrooms, and scallions, and bring to a boil. Cook for 10 minutes, then reduce the heat to a simmer and add the tofu, vegan "fish" sauce, and lime juice. Stir gently and simmer 3 minutes to heat through. Taste and adjust the seasoning. Garnish with cilantro and serve hot.

THAI COCONUT SOUP

Serves 4

This luscious soup, known as tom kha, is a favorite in Thai restaurants in the United States. Now you can make it at home.

2 cups vegetable broth

2 garlic cloves, crushed

3 dried Thai or other hot chiles, split lengthwise

1 (2-inch) piece fresh ginger, peeled and thinly sliced

1 (2-inch) piece lemongrass, white part only, crushed, or zest of 1 lemon

2 teaspoons light brown sugar, or a natural sweetener

2 (13.5-ounce) cans unsweetened coconut milk

2 cups sliced mushrooms

¼ red bell pepper, cut into slivers

8 ounces extra-firm tofu, cut into ½-inch dice

2 tablespoons Vegan "Fish" Sauce (page 220) or soy sauce

2 tablespoons lime juice

Salt and freshly ground black pepper

¼ cup chopped fresh cilantro

In a saucepan, combine the broth, garlic, chiles, ginger, and lemongrass, and bring to a boil. Reduce the heat to medium and simmer for 15 minutes to allow the flavors to blend. Strain the mixture through a fine sieve into a bowl. Discard the solids and return the liquid to the saucepan. Stir in the sugar, coconut milk, mushrooms, bell pepper, tofu, and vegan "fish" sauce. Simmer for 15 minutes, then add the lime juice and season to taste with salt and pepper. Ladle the soup into bowls and garnish with cilantro.

PAPAYA SALAD

Serves 4

Green papaya salad is refreshing and loaded with flavor. It can be served as a side salad or topped with tofu for a light main course. Omit the red pepper flakes if you don't want the heat. Vegan "fish" sauce is used in place of the native nuoc nam or nam pla.

1 large unripe papaya, peeled and shredded

1 carrot, shredded

2 scallions, minced

½ teaspoon hot red pepper flakes

2 tablespoons Vegan "Fish" Sauce (page 220)

Juice of 2 limes

1 teaspoon light brown sugar, or a natural sweetener

Salt

2 tablespoons fresh chopped cilantro

1 small ripe tomato, cut into wedges

Combine the papaya and carrot in a bowl. Add the scallions and hot red pepper flakes. Set aside.

In a small bowl, combine the "fish" sauce, lime juice, sugar, and a pinch of salt. Stir to combine, then pour over the salad and toss until well mixed. Arrange on salad plates and garnish with the cilantro and tomato wedges.

HOT AND SPICY THAI TOFU

Serves 4

If you don't have Thai chiles, use another hot chile or substitute hot red pepper flakes to taste. If you like lots of flavor but can't stand the heat, simply omit the chiles. Served over rice, this makes a nutritious and flavorful meal.

2 cups small broccoli florets

2 carrots, cut into ¼-inch slices

1 pound extra-firm tofu, drained and pressed

3 tablespoons grapeseed oil

1 small yellow onion, halved lengthwise and thinly sliced

2 to 3 fresh or dried Thai chiles, sliced lengthwise

1 garlic clove, minced

2 teaspoons light brown sugar, or a natural sweetener

3 tablespoons soy sauce

2 tablespoons Vegan "Fish" Sauce (page 220)

1 tablespoon water

2 tablespoons fresh Thai basil leaves or cilantro

2 tablespoons crushed roasted peanuts

Steam the broccoli and carrots over boiling water until almost tender, about 3 minutes. Cut the tofu into ½-inch strips and pat dry.

Heat 2 tablespoons of the oil in a large skillet over medium heat. Add the tofu, in batches if needed, and stir-fry until golden brown all over, about 10 minutes. Remove the cooked tofu to a platter and set aside.

Heat the remaining oil in the same skillet over medium heat. Add the onion and chiles and cook until tender, about 5 minutes. Add the garlic, brown sugar, soy sauce, "fish" sauce, and water. Add the reserved tofu, broccoli, and carrots and cook until hot, about 5 minutes, stirring gently to coat the tofu and vegetables with the sauce. Serve sprinkled with basil and peanuts.

BLACK PEPPER TOFU AND ASPARAGUS

Serves 4

Unlike most Thai dishes that get their heat from chiles, this one stars coarsely ground black peppercorns. For those who want extra heat, add the optional Thai chiles, but for most of us, the black pepper provides just the right amount of heat and flavor. As a variation, you can omit the asparagus or swap it out for lightly steamed broccoli florets.

14 ounces extra-firm tofu, drained and cut into 1-inch dice

⅓ cup cornstarch

2 tablespoons grapeseed oil

5 shallots, thinly sliced

6 cloves garlic, minced or pressed

8 ounces thin asparagus, cut into 1-inch pieces

1 red bell pepper, cut into thin strips

2 tablespoons grated ginger

2 Thai chiles, thinly sliced (optional)

1½ teaspoons coarsely ground black pepper

1 teaspoon sugar

2 tablespoons vegetarian oyster sauce (sometimes labeled mushroom soy sauce)

2 tablespoons soy sauce

2 tablespoons water

1 teaspoon rice vinegar

5 scallions, chopped

Hot cooked rice, to serve

Combine the tofu and cornstarch in a bowl and toss to coat. Heat the oil in a large skillet or wok over medium-high heat. Add the tofu to the hot skillet and cook until browned all over, 4 to 5 minutes. Remove the tofu from the skillet and set aside.

In the same skillet over medium heat, combine the shallots, garlic, asparagus, bell pepper, ginger, and chiles (if using). Stir-fry until the vegetables are just tender, about 5 minutes. Stir in the black pepper, sugar, oyster sauce, soy sauce, water, and vinegar. Return the tofu to skillet, add the scallions, and stir-fry until the tofu is heated through, about 2 minutes. Serve over rice.

TOFU KAPRAO

Serves 4

Kaprao is the name of a particularly fragrant and flavorful Thai basil also known as holy basil. If you can't find Thai basil (available at Asian markets) you can use another type of basil or even cilantro for a tasty enough dish, but it won't have the exact nuance of the kaprao basil. Vegetarian oyster sauce can be found in Asian markets or online. If unavailable, just add an extra tablespoon of the vegan "fish" sauce. If dried Thai chiles are unavailable, substitute 1/2 teaspoon (or more) hot red pepper flakes. Serve over freshly cooked jasmine rice.

2 tablespoons grapeseed oil

1 onion, sliced

1 red bell pepper, cut into thin strips

2 garlic cloves, minced

3 dried Thai chiles, split lengthwise

1 pound extra-firm tofu, cut into ½-inch dice

2 tablespoons soy sauce

1 tablespoon Vegan "Fish" Sauce (page 220)

1 tablespoon vegetarian oyster sauce

1 tablespoon light brown sugar, or a natural sweetener

¼ cup water or vegetable broth

1 cup Thai basil leaves, loosely packed

Heat the oil in a large skillet or wok over medium-high heat. Add the onion, bell pepper, garlic, chiles, and tofu and stir-fry until the vegetables are softened and the tofu is golden, about 5 minutes. Stir in the soy sauce, "fish" sauce, vegetarian oyster sauce, sugar, and water, stirring to coat. Stir in the basil leaves and stir-fry until wilted. Serve hot.

TOFU WITH THAI PEANUT SAUCE

Serves 4

An alternate way to serve this scrumptious dish is to cut the tofu into 1-inch cubes, fry it, and serve with a bowl of Thai peanut sauce on the side for dipping.

1 tablespoon grapeseed oil

1 pound extra-firm tofu, cut in ½-inch strips

1 tablespoon minced garlic

½ cup chopped scallions

1 tablespoon chopped fresh ginger

1 tablespoon soy sauce

1 tablespoon dry sherry

1 teaspoon light brown sugar, or a natural sweetener

1 (8-ounce) can sliced bamboo shoots, drained and rinsed

¼ cup unsalted peanuts, chopped

Spicy Peanut Sauce (page 199)

Freshly cooked rice

Heat the oil in a large skillet over medium-high heat. Add the tofu, garlic, scallions, and ginger and cook for 5 minutes. Add the soy sauce, sherry, sugar, bamboo shoots, and peanuts, and mix well. Add the peanut sauce and stir gently until well combined. Cook for 5 minutes or until hot. Serve at once over freshly cooked rice.

SPICY PEANUT SAUCE

Makes about 1 cup

In addition to its use in the preceding recipe, this also makes a good dipping sauce for spring rolls, steamed broccoli, or just about anything.

½ cup creamy peanut butter

¼ cup water

3 tablespoons soy sauce

2 teaspoons light brown sugar, or a natural sweetener

1 tablespoon fresh lime juice

1 tablespoon rice vinegar

1½ teaspoons Asian chili paste

In a small bowl or food processor, combine all the ingredients and mix until well blended. Taste to adjust seasoning. Use at once, or cover and refrigerate until needed.

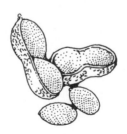

RED CURRY PASTE

Makes about 3/4 cup

This curry paste can be used as a base for Thai red curries as well as an addition to sauces, stir-fries, marinades, soups, and stews. Refrigerated and tightly covered, it will keep for 2 weeks.

8 dried red Thai or other hot red chiles
1 teaspoon whole white peppercorns
1 teaspoon coriander seeds
½ teaspoon cumin seeds
¼ cup chopped onion
2 tablespoons chopped garlic
2 tablespoons thinly sliced fresh lemongrass white part only, or zest of 1 lemon
1 tablespoon chopped fresh cilantro
2 teaspoons chopped fresh ginger
1 teaspoon finely grated lime zest
2 teaspoons sweet paprika
½ teaspoon ground nutmeg
2 tablespoons grapeseed oil

Wearing rubber gloves, stem and seed the chiles and cut into ½-inch pieces. Soak for 20 minutes in a bowl with enough hot water to cover. Drain the chiles, reserving 1 tablespoon of the soaking liquid.

Place the peppercorns, coriander, and cumin seeds in a small skillet over medium heat, stirring until fragrant, being careful not to burn them. Cool the spices and finely grind them in a blender or an electric spice grinder.

In a food processor, purée the chiles to a paste with the reserved soaking liquid and the ground spices. Add the onion, garlic, lemongrass, cilantro, ginger, lime zest, paprika, nutmeg, and oil and process until smooth. Keep the curry paste tightly covered in the refrigerator.

QUICK THAI-STYLE CURRY SAUCE

Makes about 2¹/₂ cups

This easy but nontraditional sauce was born out of a lack of time and ingredients coupled with a craving for a Thai-flavored sauce. Use it to transform stir-fried vegetables or tofu into a fragrant feast.

4 dried Thai chiles, or 2 teaspoons hot red pepper flakes

2 garlic cloves, minced

1 tablespoon grated fresh ginger

2 tablespoons curry powder

1 tablespoon light brown sugar, or a natural sweetener

1 teaspoon paprika

1 teaspoon ground coriander

½ teaspoon ground cumin

2 tablespoons grapeseed oil

1 tablespoon soy sauce

¼ cup water

2 tablespoons fresh lime juice

1 (13.5-ounce) can unsweetened coconut milk

Cut the chiles into small pieces and place in a heatproof bowl. Cover with boiling water and soak for 15 minutes. Drain the chiles and place them in a blender or food processor. Add the garlic, ginger, curry powder, sugar, paprika, coriander, and cumin, and blend to a paste. Add the oil, soy sauce, and water and blend until smooth. Pour the mixture into a saucepan and bring to a boil. Reduce the heat to low and simmer for 5 minutes, stirring frequently to prevent scorching. Remove from the heat and stir in the lime juice and as much of the coconut milk as needed to make a smooth sauce. If using right away, heat until hot over low heat, stirring, or set aside to cool, then cover and refrigerate until ready to use.

THAI LIME VINAIGRETTE

Makes 1 cup

The basic vinaigrette of Southeast Asia is perfect as a dipping sauce and for tossing with salads or cooked vegetables.

½ cup fresh lime juice

2 tablespoons soy sauce

3 tablespoons light brown sugar, or a natural sweetener

1 crushed dried red Thai chile, or ½ teaspoon hot red pepper flakes

1 large garlic clove, crushed

In a bowl, combine all the ingredients, whisking until well blended. Allow to stand 15 minutes at room temperature before serving.

SEITAN SATAYS WITH GINGER-PEANUT SAUCE

Serves 4

Seitan is sturdy enough to thread easily onto skewers to make these tasty satays. Traditionally served as an appetizer, it can also be served as a main dish.

1 pound seitan, cut into ¼-inch slices

½ cup water

4 tablespoons soy sauce

1 tablespoon plus 1 teaspoon light brown sugar, or a natural sweetener

1 garlic clove, minced

1 cup vegetable broth

⅓ cup peanut butter

2 teaspoons minced fresh ginger

1 tablespoon fresh lime juice

¼ teaspoon cayenne

Orange slices

Thread the seitan slices onto bamboo or metal skewers, pushing down firmly. Blend the water, 3 tablespoons of the soy sauce, 1 tablespoon of the brown sugar, and the garlic in a shallow baking dish. Add the skewered seitan and marinate for an hour, turning once.

While the seitan is marinating, combine the broth, peanut butter, ginger, lime juice, remaining 1 tablespoon of soy sauce, remaining 1 teaspoon of brown sugar, and the cayenne in a blender or food processor, and blend until smooth. Transfer the mixture to a saucepan and simmer until thick enough to coat a spoon, stirring constantly, about 10 minutes.

Preheat the broiler or grill. Cook the satays until hot and browned, about 3 minutes per side. Arrange the satays on a platter and garnish with orange slices. Pour the sauce into individual dipping bowls to serve.

KOREAN BEAN SPROUT SALAD

Serves 4

This refreshing and crunchy salad is a traditional accompaniment to Korean barbecue, but I find it complements most Asian meals. It's best to add the dressing at the last minute to keep the bean sprouts as crisp as possible.

3 tablespoons dark sesame oil

3 tablespoons rice vinegar

¼ teaspoon salt

½ teaspoon hot red pepper flakes

8 ounces fresh bean sprouts

3 minced scallions

1 tablespoon toasted sesame seeds

In a small bowl, combine the oil, vinegar, salt, and red pepper flakes until well blended.

Place the bean sprouts in a bowl. Add the scallions and the dressing and toss lightly to combine. Spoon the salad into small bowls and sprinkle the sesame seeds on top.

ASPARAGUS DAIKON SALAD

Serves 4

Daikon is a large, white, carrot-shaped radish with a mild flavor. It is popular throughout Asia, where it is served raw or cooked. If asparagus is not available, substitute broccoli or cauliflower florets.

1 pound asparagus, tough ends trimmed

1 cup daikon, cut into matchstick julienne

3 garlic cloves, minced

1 tablespoon grated fresh ginger

½ teaspoon salt

½ teaspoon sugar, or a natural sweetener

2 tablespoons soy sauce

2 teaspoons dark sesame oil

1 tablespoon rice vinegar

¼ teaspoon cayenne

Slice the asparagus into matchsticks by cutting each stalk into 3-inch lengths, then cutting the lengths into thin strips with a sharp paring knife. Steam the asparagus until tender-crisp, about 2 minutes.

Combine the daikon, garlic, ginger, salt, sugar, soy sauce, sesame oil, vinegar, and cayenne in a large bowl. Add the warm asparagus and let the salad stand for 10 minutes at room temperature before serving.

INDONESIAN TEMPEH SALAD

Serves 4

Since tempeh originated in Indonesia, it should come as no surprise that some of the best ways to prepare it come out of that part of the world as well.

1 (8-ounce) package tempeh

3 tablespoons rice vinegar

2 tablespoons peanut butter

1 tablespoon dark sesame oil

1 tablespoon hot chili oil

½ teaspoon Asian chili paste

2 tablespoons soy sauce

1 cup snow peas, trimmed and blanched

1 cup bean sprouts

1 (8-ounce) can sliced water chestnuts, drained and rinsed

1 cup grated carrot

3 scallions, chopped

¼ cup chopped peanuts

Shredded romaine lettuce

Poach the tempeh in simmering water for 30 minutes. Drain and chop the tempeh. Set aside.

In a shallow bowl, combine the vinegar, peanut butter, sesame oil, chili oil, chili paste, and soy sauce. Add the reserved tempeh and toss to coat well. Cover and refrigerate for 1 hour.

In a large bowl, combine the snow peas, bean sprouts, water chestnuts, carrot, scallions, and peanuts. Add the marinated tempeh and the dressing and toss well to combine. Serve on a bed of shredded lettuce.

JAPANESE EGGPLANT SALAD

Serves 4

Japanese eggplants are smaller and sweeter than those grown in the West. They can be found in Asian grocery stores and well-stocked supermarkets. If unavailable, use a regular eggplant.

3 Japanese eggplants, trimmed and halved lengthwise

2 tablespoons grapeseed oil

½ teaspoon hot red pepper flakes

1 cup vegetable broth

2 tablespoons soy sauce

2 tablespoons dry sherry

1 tablespoon dark sesame oil

1 tablespoon sugar, or a natural sweetener

1 teaspoon cornstarch mixed with 1 tablespoon water

1 teaspoon grated fresh ginger

4 tablespoons rice vinegar

¼ teaspoon minced garlic

8 ounces romaine lettuce, cut crosswise into 1-inch strips

6 ounces fresh snow peas, blanched 1 minute in boiling salted water

¼ cup thinly sliced red bell pepper

¼ cup thinly sliced daikon

Cut the eggplant halves into ½-inch-thick slices. Heat the grapeseed oil in a large skillet over medium-high heat. Add the eggplant slices and red pepper flakes. Stir-fry for about 5 minutes, or until the eggplant slices are lightly browned on both sides. Add the broth, soy sauce, sherry, sesame oil, and sugar. Cover and reduce the heat to medium. Simmer until the eggplant is just tender, about 5 minutes. Use a slotted spoon to transfer the eggplant to a platter and set aside. Strain the cooking liquid, reserving ¾ cup.

Boil the reserved liquid in the skillet until reduced to ½ cup. Stir in the cornstarch mixture and cook, stirring constantly, until the sauce is thickened. Pour the sauce into a small bowl along with any liquid from the eggplant. Add the ginger, rice vinegar, and garlic. Set aside and allow to come to room temperature. Arrange the lettuce on a large platter. In a bowl, combine ¼ cup of the reserved sauce with the snow peas, red bell pepper, and daikon and toss to coat. Arrange the vegetable mixture on top of the lettuce. Top with the eggplant, and spoon the remaining sauce over the salad.

KOREAN CUCUMBER SALAD

Serves 4

This salad is best served soon after being made. Wait too long, and the cucumbers will lose their crispness.

1 English cucumber, peeled, halved lengthwise, and seeded

1 scallion, chopped

1 garlic clove, minced

½ teaspoon chopped fresh ginger

½ teaspoon salt

⅛ teaspoon cayenne

Pinch sugar, or a natural sweetener

3 tablespoons rice vinegar

Cut the cucumber into ½-inch-thick slices and place them in a bowl. Add the scallion, garlic, ginger, salt, cayenne, sugar, and vinegar. Mix well, then cover and refrigerate until chilled.

KIMCHI

Serves 8 to 12

This classic Korean condiment of sweet, sour, and spicy-tasting pickled vegetables will keep about 2 weeks if stored properly in the refrigerator.

1 cup water

1 cup red wine vinegar

1 cup sugar, or a natural sweetener

⅓ cup dry sherry

½ teaspoon salt

½ tablespoon minced fresh ginger

3 dried hot red chiles, split lengthwise

2 celery ribs, cut in ½-inch diagonal slices

2 carrots, cut in ½-inch diagonal slices

1 small zucchini, cut in ½-inch diagonal slices

½ red bell pepper, cut in ½-inch dice

2 scallions, chopped

Heat the water, vinegar, sugar, sherry, and salt in a saucepan and bring to a boil. Reduce the heat to low and simmer for 5 minutes. Remove from the heat and cool to room temperature. Stir in the ginger and chiles. Place the celery, carrots, zucchini, bell pepper, and scallions in a 1-quart glass jar or bowl with a tight-fitting lid. Ladle the vinegar mixture into the jar, and store, tightly sealed, in the refrigerator for at least 2 days before serving.

COLD BUCKWHEAT NOODLES WITH JADE VEGETABLES

Serves 4

Buckwheat noodles, or soba, are popular in Japan, where they are used in soups, sautéed with vegetables, or served cold as in this recipe.

2 teaspoons minced garlic

2 teaspoons grated fresh ginger

2 teaspoons grated orange zest

4 tablespoons grapeseed oil

2 tablespoons rice vinegar

1 tablespoon tamari soy sauce

1 tablespoon dark sesame oil

1 teaspoon Sriracha sauce

¼ cup finely chopped green bell pepper

3 cups chopped bok choy

1 zucchini, cut into ½-inch dice

2 tablespoons chopped scallion

8 ounces buckwheat noodles or soba

In a food processor, pulse the garlic, ginger, and orange zest until well mixed. With the machine running, add 3 tablespoons of the grapeseed oil, vinegar, tamari, sesame oil, and Sriracha sauce and mix until well blended. Set aside.

Heat the remaining 1 tablespoon grapeseed oil in a large skillet or wok over medium-high heat. Add the bell pepper, bok choy, zucchini, and scallion. Stir-fry for 3 minutes to soften, then stir in the reserved sauce mixture, and cook, stirring for 3 minutes longer. Remove from the heat. Taste to adjust seasonings.

Cook the noodles in a large pot of boiling water until just tender, stirring occasionally. Drain, and rinse under cold water. Drain well so that no water remains on the noodles. Add the noodles to the vegetable mixture, tossing gently to combine. Transfer to a large bowl. Cover and refrigerate until chilled.

VIETNAMESE NOODLES WITH TEMPEH AND PEANUTS

Serves 4

The hottest Vietnamese dishes will be found in the South, where cooks make more liberal use of chiles than their Northern counterparts.

1 (8-ounce) package tempeh

2 tablespoons grapeseed oil

¼ cup soy sauce (or Vegan "Fish" Sauce, page 220)

3 tablespoons rice vinegar

1½ tablespoons sugar, or a natural sweetener

1 tablespoon hoisin sauce

2 teaspoons hot chili oil

8 ounces rice noodles or linguine

1 carrot, shredded

1 bunch scallions, minced

2 tablespoons minced fresh cilantro

½ cup crushed dry-roasted peanuts

Poach the tempeh in simmering water for 30 minutes. Drain and cut into ½-inch strips. Heat the oil in a large skillet or wok over medium-high heat. Add the tempeh and cook until browned, about 10 minutes. Transfer to a large bowl.

In a small bowl, combine the soy sauce, vinegar, sugar, hoisin sauce, and chili oil. Pour the mixture onto the tempeh and set aside.

Cook the noodles according to package directions. About 3 minutes before the noodles are done, add the carrots to the pot and finish cooking. Drain the noodles and carrots well, and add to the tempeh mixture. Add the scallions, cilantro, and peanuts, tossing gently to combine. Taste and adjust seasoning, adding more chili oil if desired. Serve warm or at room temperature.

INDONESIAN COCONUT RICE

Serves 4

Coconut-flavored rice is a one-dish feast. For special occasions, Indonesians mold it into a tower and garnish it with vegetables, peanuts, or toasted coconut. Reduce or omit the red pepper flakes for a milder version.

2 tablespoons grapeseed oil

1 yellow onion, minced

3 garlic cloves, minced

4 scallions minced

1 tablespoon grated fresh ginger

1 teaspoon ground turmeric

1 teaspoon ground cinnamon

½ teaspoon hot red pepper flakes

1 teaspoon dry mustard

¼ teaspoon ground cloves

1 tablespoon sugar, or a natural sweetener

4 cups cooked long-grain rice

1 cup shredded coconut

Salt and freshly ground black pepper

Heat the oil in a large skillet over medium-high heat, add the onion and garlic and cook until softened, about 5 minutes. Add the scallions, ginger, turmeric, cinnamon, red pepper flakes, mustard, cloves, and sugar, and cook, stirring constantly, for 2 minutes. Add the rice and stir to mix evenly. Gently stir in the coconut. Season to taste with salt and pepper, and heat until hot. Cover, and set aside for 5 minutes before serving.

VEGETABLE PANCIT

Serves 4

Pancit is the Filipino word for noodle. If Filipino-style pancit noodles are unavailable, substitute angel hair pasta.

8 ounces pancit noodles or angel hair pasta

2 tablespoons grapeseed oil

1 red onion, thinly sliced

2 garlic cloves, minced

3 scallions, minced

2 cups shredded cabbage

1 large carrot, shredded

¼ cup water

2 tablespoons soy sauce

1 tablespoon tomato paste

1 teaspoon Asian chili oil

Freshly ground black pepper

Lime wedges

Cook the noodles according to package directions. Drain and set aside.

Heat the oil in a large skillet or wok over medium-high heat. Add the onion, garlic, scallions, cabbage, and carrot, and stir-fry for 5 minutes.

In a small bowl, combine the water, soy sauce, tomato paste, and chili oil, stirring to blend. Add to the vegetables, cover, and cook 2 minutes longer.

Add the cooked noodles and toss to combine. Season with a generous amount of black pepper to taste and add additional soy sauce, if desired. Cook until hot, then transfer to a serving platter and garnish with lime wedges.

MALAYSIAN REMPEH TEMPEH

Serves 4

Rempeh is a Malaysian seasoning made of chiles, garlic, ginger, and shallots. I couldn't resist the rhyme of pairing rempeh with tempeh. Serve over rice.

1 pound tempeh, cut into ½-inch cubes

2 to 3 slender red chiles, seeded and chopped

2 shallots, chopped

3 garlic cloves

2 teaspoons grated ginger

2 tablespoons tomato ketchup

1 tablespoon fresh lime juice

1 tablespoon soy sauce

1 tablespoon water

1 teaspoon light brown sugar, or a natural sweetener

3 tablespoons grapeseed oil

¼ cup chopped fresh basil or cilantro

Poach or steam the tempeh for 30 minutes. Drain and set aside.

In a food processor, combine the chiles, shallots, garlic, and ginger and process to a paste. Set aside.

In a small bowl, combine the ketchup, lime juice, soy sauce, water, and sugar. Mix well and set aside.

Heat the oil in a large skillet over medium heat. Add the reserved tempeh and cook until golden brown all over, stirring occasionally, about 10 minutes. Stir in the reserved chili paste and cook until fragrant, about 2 minutes. Stir in the reserved sauce and continue to cook until the tempeh is coated and the flavors are well blended, about 5 minutes. Stir in the basil, just prior to serving.

JAPANESE SOBA NOODLES

Serves 4

This Japanese dish of hearty buckwheat noodles and crisp stir-fried vegetables in a spicy-sweet sauce is one of my husband's favorites.

12 ounces buckwheat soba noodles

¼ cup soy sauce

1 tablespoon light brown sugar, or a natural sweetener

2 tablespoons dry sherry

2 tablespoons dark sesame oil

1 tablespoon rice vinegar

1 teaspoon minced fresh ginger

1 garlic clove, minced

¼ teaspoon cayenne

2 teaspoons cornstarch

1 tablespoon grapeseed oil

1 red bell pepper, cut into strips

2 cups finely shredded cabbage

¼ cup sliced scallions

2 tablespoons toasted sesame seeds

2 tablespoons minced fresh parsley

Cook the soba noodles according to package directions. Drain and set aside.

In a shallow bowl, combine the soy sauce, sugar, sherry, sesame oil, vinegar, ginger, garlic, and cayenne. Blend in the cornstarch and set aside.

Heat the grapeseed oil in a large skillet over medium-high heat. Add the bell pepper, cabbage, and scallions, and cook until tender, about 5 minutes. Add the reserved sauce and cook 2 minutes longer, stirring to thicken. Add the reserved soba noodles, tossing to coat and heat through. Serve garnished with sesame seeds and parsley.

215

KOREAN RICE AND MILLET

Serves 4

Koreans traditionally serve rice at every meal, either alone or combined with beans or another grain, such as millet, which has a delicate, nutty flavor. This dish can be made spicier by increasing the amount of spicy chili paste known as gochujang, but I prefer it mildly spiced since I like to serve it with spicy-hot stir-fried vegetables.

1 cup rice

½ cup millet

3 cups vegetable broth

1 to 2 tablespoons gochujang (Korean chili paste)

1 teaspoon toasted sesame oil

Salt and freshly ground black pepper

1 tablespoon chopped fresh cilantro or parsley

1 tablespoon toasted sesame seeds

In a large saucepan, bring the rice, millet, and broth to a boil. Reduce the heat to low, cover, and simmer for 30 minutes, or until the water is absorbed. Remove the pan from the heat, add the gochujang and sesame oil and season to taste with salt and pepper. Fluff with a fork and cover for 5 minutes. Transfer to a bowl and garnish with cilantro and toasted sesame seeds.

DAIKON WALNUT CONDIMENT

Makes about 1½ cups

This deliciously spicy condiment from Indonesia is especially good served with rice or noodle dishes.

½ cup walnut pieces

1 cup sliced, peeled daikon

1 small fresh hot green chile, halved and seeded

½ teaspoon sugar, or a natural sweetener

½ teaspoon salt

1 teaspoon cider vinegar

Preheat the oven to 350°F. Spread the walnuts on a baking sheet. Bake until lightly toasted, about 10 minutes.

In a food processor, chop the daikon and chile in short bursts. Add the walnuts, sugar, and salt and coarsely chop. Blend in the vinegar.

Transfer to a jar or bowl with tight-fitting lid and refrigerate until ready to serve.

WASABI MISO DRESSING

Makes about ³/₄ cup

This Japanese-inspired dressing uses wasabi, the fiery green horseradish served with sushi. Miso paste is a nutritious fermented soybean paste available at natural food stores and Asian grocery stores.

2 teaspoons white miso paste
1 tablespoon soy sauce
2 tablespoons mirin
1 teaspoon sugar, or a natural sweetener
¾ teaspoon wasabi powder
1 garlic clove, minced
½ teaspoon finely grated fresh ginger
⅓ cup grapeseed oil

In a small bowl, combine the miso and soy sauce and blend until smooth. Stir in the mirin, sugar, wasabi, garlic, ginger, and oil until well blended. Taste and adjust seasoning.

TAMARI VINAIGRETTE

Makes about 2/3 cup

This salad dressing also makes a great light dipping sauce for Japanese tempura.

¼ cup grapeseed oil

2 tablespoons tamari or soy sauce

2 tablespoons rice wine vinegar

1 tablespoon dark sesame oil

¼ teaspoon hot red pepper flakes

Combine all the ingredients in a small bowl and mix until well blended. Refrigerate tightly covered in a small bowl or jar.

Note: Tamari is a high-quality soy sauce used in Asian cooking. When tamari isn't available, any good-quality soy sauce can be used in its place. For those watching their sodium, look for reduced-sodium varieties of tamari and soy sauce.

VEGAN "FISH" SAUCE

Makes about 3/4 cup

Known as nuoc nam in Vietnam and nam pla in Thailand, this sauce is traditionally used in much the same way soy sauce or tamari is used in China or Japan. I like the extra dimension this sauce gives to a recipe, although, in a pinch, you could get by with substituting a good-quality soy sauce or tamari.

½ cup soy sauce

2 garlic cloves, minced

½ teaspoon hot red pepper flakes

1 tablespoon fresh lemon juice

1 tablespoon sugar, or a natural sweetener

¼ cup water

Combine all the ingredients in a small jar with a tight-fitting lid. Shake until well blended. Store the jar in the refrigerator.

Index

ACKNOWLEDGMENTS

I am grateful to many friends and family members who shared their time and talents to help make this book possible. Special thanks goes to Sangeeta Kumar, Patty Gershanik, Marie Lange, and Carole Lazur for sharing their personal recipes, and to Robin Dempsey, Laura Frisk, and Linda Levy for their diligent recipe testing. I'm also grateful to Carol and Francis Janes, Tal Ronnen, and Samantha Ragan for their input.

Thank you to my husband Jon Robertson and his company Vegan Heritage Press for publishing *Vegan Fire & Spice*, and to Kirsty Melville and everyone involved at Andrews McMeel Publishing for giving this work a new look, a new title, and a new home, especially editor Grace Suh, as well as Holly Ogden, Maureen Sullivan, and Carol Coe.

ABOUT THE AUTHOR

ROBIN ROBERTSON is a vegan chef and award-winning cookbook author whose culinary experience spans nearly thirty years. She has been a chef, caterer, cooking teacher, and food columnist. Her best-selling cookbooks include *Quick-Fix Vegan, Quick-Fix Vegetarian, Vegan Planet, Fresh from the Vegan Slow Cooker,* and *One-Dish Vegan.* Robin's features and columns appear regularly in *VegNews Magazine, Vegetarian Times, Cooking Light, Natural Health,* and other magazines. Robin works from her home, an 1833 farmhouse in the Shenandoah Valley of Virginia that she shares with her husband Jon, four cats, and more ducks than she can count. Follow Robin on Facebook (robin.robertson.712) and Twitter (@globalvegan), as well as on her website www.robinrobertson.com.

OTHER BOOKS BY
ROBIN ROBERTSON

Robin Robertson's
VEGAN WITHOUT BORDERS
shows how to make
culinary borders disappear
when you use plant-based
ingredients to make 150
of her favorite recipes
from around the world.

THE NUT BUTTER COOKBOOK
Think outside the jar with these
luscious recipes enriched with the
flavor and nutrition of nut butter.

QUICK-FIX VEGETARIAN provides
busy families with 150 practical
vegetarian dishes that can be
prepared in less time than it takes
to have a pizza delivered.

QUICK-FIX VEGAN includes 150
fast and easy vegan recipes all made
in 30 minutes or less from a well-
loved, best-selling author in the
vegan community.

MORE QUICK-FIX VEGAN delivers
150 new recipes, tips, and time-
saving strategies, including making
convenience foods from scratch to
save you time and money.

HOT VEGAN

Andrews McMeel Publishing, LLC
an Andrews McMeel Universal company
1130 Walnut Street, Kansas City, Missouri 64106

www.andrewsmcmeel.com

14 15 16 17 18 RR2 10 9 8 7 6 5 4 3 2 1

ISBN: 978-1-4494-6007-5

Library of Congress Control Number: 2014935719

Cover photo: iStock
Editor: Grace Suh
Designer: Holly Ogden
Art director: Julie Barnes
Production manager: Carol Coe
Production editor: Maureen Sullivan
Demand planner: Sue Eikos

ATTENTION: SCHOOLS AND BUSINESSES
Andrews McMeel books are available at quantity discounts with bulk purchase for educational, business, or sales promotional use. For information, please e-mail the Andrews McMeel Publishing Special Sales Department:
specialsales@amuniversal.com